Falling Perfectly
WITHOUT TRYING

A TRUE STORY

Jenny Duhaylonsod Delos Santos

Praise for *Falling Perfectly Without Trying*

"Domestic violence is sometimes seen as one large social problem, but this book reminds us that every woman's story is different, and seldom exists in isolation. Falling Perfectly Without Trying is the passionate recounting of resilience and recovery in the face of enormous challenges—the human spirit can survive even when the odds are against us."
—Virginia McCullough, Award-winning Author of *Amber Light*

"Jenny Delos Santos gives an open, honest depiction of how challenging domestic violence is; how victims suffer from mental health and substance abuse issues because of the domestic terrorism they experience. She made herself so vulnerable because it's clear she has a true desire to help other domestic violence victims."
—Marci Lopes, Deputy Director, Domestic Violence Action Center

"In her memoir, *Falling Perfectly Without Trying,* Jenny Delos Santos has shared a deeply personal account of how she overcame domestic abuse and the deep scars it leaves behind. Her story is filled with incredible pain yet at the same time tremendous courage and hope that readers will find inspiration from. It touched my heart and so will it yours."
—Simi K. Rao, Physician and Author of *The Accidental Wife*

"Jenny Delos Santos' highly personal tale is at once heart-wrenching and inspiring. To learn that she endured such abuse and hardship was heart-rending, and I hope that by her sharing her story, it will help those enduring domestic abuse to find the help they need to end the cycle and emerge victorious, as she did. More importantly though, I hope her story is one that can inspire others to overcome."

—Erika Engle, Columnist and Reporter, *Honolulu Star-Advertiser*

"Jenny Delos Santos' story illuminates her will to survive and her trials of life as an emotionally-abused wife and mother, and the steps she took to turn her life from one of failure to victor. *Falling Perfectly Without Trying* will make you an advocate for people who suffer from domestic violence."

—Valerie Jean Routhieaux, Author of the Colonial America series

"Jenny Delos Santos' first book, Falling Perfectly Without Trying, can be compared to a great mystery novel. Based on her life story, it grabs you from the moment you read the first paragraph and takes you on an emotional roller coaster ride filled with many twists and turns, and ups and downs. She shares her hopes and dreams, as well as her challenges from domestic abuse, mental health issues, and cancer. When she falls down, she gets back up, dusts herself off and continues towards her dream of happiness for herself and her children. Thank you, Jenny Delos Santos, for having the strength and giving others hope as they face their own challenges and struggles. You are an inspiration and have shown us if we "Don't Quit" that we can also survive. A must-read memoir I could not put down and kept turning the pages until I reached the end!"

—Charles Mole Jr., Former District Director of District 49 Toastmasters and Police Dispatcher for the Honolulu Police Department

A TRUE STORY
Jenny Duhaylonsod Delos Santos

Green Bay, WI 54311

Falling Perfectly Without Trying by Jenny Duhaylonsod Delos Santos, © Copyright 2018 by Jenny Duhaylonsod Delos Santos. Author Photo taken by Christina Chun. All photos used within the book courtesy of the Delos Santos family.

This book is a true story about the real life of Jenny Duhaylonsod Delos Santos of Honolulu, Hawai'i. All names and locations are real, except when changed to protect the identities of individuals who wished to remain anonymous. Permission has been obtained where possible for the use of names in the book. This book reflects the opinions of the author and her life's decisions. Written Dreams Publishing does not approve, condone, or disapprove of these opinions.

All rights reserved. In accordance with the U.S. Copyright Act of 1976, no part of this publication may be reproduced, distributed, or transmitted in any form or by any means, or stored in a database or retrieval system, without prior written permission of the publisher, Written Dreams Publishing, Green Bay, Wisconsin 54311. Please be aware that if you've received this book with a "stripped" off cover, please know that the publisher and the author may not have received payment for this book, and that it has been reported as stolen property. Please visit www.writtendreams.com to see more of the unique books published by Written Dreams Publishing.

Publishing Editor: Brittiany Koren
Copy-editor: Maria Connor
Cover Art Designer: Sunny Fassbender
Interior Layout Designer: Amanda Dix

Category: Nonfiction Memoir-Domestic Abuse/Cancer
Description: A Hawaiian woman perseveres to survive domestic abuse, mental illness, and cancer.
Paperback ISBN: 978-1-7326919-6-4
Ebook ISBN: 978-1-7326919-7-1
LOCN: Catalog info applied for.
First Edition published by Written Dreams Publishing in November, 2018.

Green Bay, WI 54311

This book is dedicated to my two children, my husband Pancho, my parents and siblings, co-workers, and friends at the daily newspaper, Marci Lopes, Charles Mole Jr., District 49 Toastmasters and Sisters in Crime/Hawai'i members, my LCC English teacher Dayle Turner, and the late U.S. Congressman K. Mark Takai, who have all been very supportive of me.
Thank You All So Much!

I have written this book to offer hope in today's world. **Falling Perfectly Without Trying** *is my gift to all of you.*

Dear Reader,

I wrote this book because I wanted to give others hope to keep on going no matter how hard life may be.
At fifty-eight-years old, I felt like I'd been through so much in my life that I wanted to share with all of you what I've experienced so that you will know you are not alone—even with overcoming despair, depression, life's obstacles, struggles, or sadness.
I'm not a professional employee in the health industry or a social worker who has mastered the topic of domestic violence. I'm a clerk at the daily newspaper, and I like to read and write. I wrote this originally with all real names, but later changed some people's names to protect their identities in my story.
While this is a true recounting of my own personal journey, I hope you find comfort that you can get out of any situation and make a better life for yourself, as I did. It is for you that I share this. I hope you enjoy my story and find inspiration.

Jenny Delos Santos
November, 2018

For every pain that we must bear,
For every burden, every care,
There's a reason.
For every grief that bows the head,
For every teardrop that is shed,
There's a reason.
For every hurt, for every plight,
For every lonely, pain-wracked night,
There's a reason.
But if we trust God as we should,
It will all work out for the Good,
God knows the reason.
               —Anonymous

Preface

In the summer of 2008, I learned that the month of October is Domestic Violence Awareness Month. Because of my experience with domestic violence in the past, I wanted to write an editorial article about the subject. I knew the main editor and assistant editor of the Editorial Department of the daily newspaper very well, and I knew they would let me submit an editorial piece.

As a result, in October 2008, I had a mission to jam my life story into 500 words—the maximum word count allowed for the editorial page. At first, I thought it was impossible. So many unexpected things had happened in my life, and there was so much I wanted to share with others. While it was difficult, I somehow managed to get the most important facts onto paper.

I couldn't go into detail about the reason why I left my ex-husband at a moment's notice. I had been so determined not to leave him for multiple reasons.

In the article, I also couldn't explain the many mental illnesses I'd been diagnosed with due to the traumatic experiences and mental abuse that my ex-husband had put me through, including being threatened and interrogated by him on a daily basis. My ex-husband had never hit me, but he had shoved me enough times to cause bruising.

According to *Intimate Violence Against Women* edited by Paula K. Lundberg-Love and Shelley L. Marmion, the book mentioned that emotional abuse is the worse abuse, especially since it's so hard to identify, and you can't press charges against someone who've used emotional abuse against their significant other.

Emotional abuse is when a person puts another person down, calls their significant other all kinds of names, say and do things to make another person feel bad about themselves and even when a person threatens their significant other.

As I wrote the editorial article, I knew I couldn't go into detail about how domestic violence had affected my two children, Michael and Remie. By the time I was writing the end of the article, I mentioned that Remie had PTSD. It was such a vague description of what we dealt with after all three of us returned to my parents' home in O'ahu, Hawai'i.

I'm not sure how much the domestic abuse affected my son after we left Vallejo, California. It's a suspicion of mine that he desperately needed psychiatric help. My ex-husband, Miguel disagreed. He doesn't believe our children need to see a psychiatrist, including receiving medicine to help. He believes the Lord has cured them.

At the Queen's Medical Center Day Treatment Services outpatient classes I attended, the counselors said that a person can be diagnosed with mental illness due to traumatic experiences; however, it depends if they were genetically dispositioned. The individual can be fine while growing up, but when they are in their twenties, the mental illness could appear due to environmental factors, including stress, poverty, and other hardships that can act as a trigger and increase the person's risk of developing a mental illness disease.

There were other reasons why I wrote the article. Those of us who have experienced domestic abuse rarely have the opportunity to share our story about what happens *after* the tragic occurrence. There are many stories of women and men being abused by their significant others, and sometimes it leads to death. But many people don't know what happens to domestic abuse survivors or their children after they've moved on out of the situation.

I also wanted to eliminate the stereotype of people misusing welfare and government assistance. While few welfare recipients *are* dishonest with food stamps and monetary assistance, there are thousands more who need the help and never misuse it. Whatever the circumstances, the recipients all seem to be grouped into one class and judged harshly. By telling my story, I hoped to alleviate some of the discrimination as well as society's skewed perceptions.

I had to condense my article into just 500 words. How much can a person say about their life in that many words? So much can be left unsaid or unexplained.

When I finally finished writing the article, the editor and assistant editor had to condense it even more. After a few days of editing and rewrites, my story was printed on Sunday, Oct. 26, 2008, in the daily newspaper. The headline read: Despite all odds.

I read the published article at home for the first time. I was satisfied, but all I could think of was what would people think of me, particularly my coworkers. I was worried that they may think less of me or even make fun of my circumstances.

On Monday (the day after the article was printed), I went to work. I was shocked by what happened minutes after I entered the building. Many of my co-workers came up to me and hugged me. They were sympathetic, concerned, and couldn't believe that I—someone they knew—had experienced domestic abuse.

More than ten years have passed since I wrote that article. I'd grappled with the idea of writing a book to tell everything in detail so that there were no questions left unanswered for quite a long time. A few people asked me "Are you sure you want the whole world to find out about what happened in your life?"

I admit I've had second thoughts, but I was determined to write my story despite all the negativity.

I had spoken to my managing editor of the newsroom if I could apply for the position of a reporter. I felt I was physically and mentally ready to move on, and capable of handling all the responsibilities of a reporter. I was told that the editors needed more experienced journalists at that time.

I couldn't give up. Armed with all the reasons why I left Miguel, I needed to get my story out there into the public's eye, determined to help others in similar situations. My own journey was unpredictable. Fleeing a horrible nightmare, walking on a rocky road to a better life, and envisioning dreams and goals that helped me to overcome all the obstacles and all challenges that came my way.

I had no idea I would be faced with many more obstacles after leaving Miguel. It surprised me when life took a sharp right turn, then a sharp left, and I ended up walking on a steep hill. But, here I am still not giving up.

***

It took me two and a half years to write this book. There were many nights I stayed up until 2 AM, trying to get just one more paragraph written. I'd go to work tired, yawning and drinking a can of caffeine to wake me up. The best time for me to write was between 9 PM to the early morning hours, because the house would be quiet. I could concentrate so much better and the words would come easier.

I thought it would be smooth sailing, because I would be concentrating on writing about myself. But it wasn't. It was emotional, sometimes typing through the tears of writing the words to my experiences. There was a lot of pain and hurt and disbelief—even after I knew I was in a safe environment.

Shortly after making the decision to write my memoir, I found out there were Toastmasters meetings held at Restaurant Row where my workplace was located. Toastmasters is a group that gets together to improve each other's speech skills and leadership skills. By giving speeches, gaining feedback as well as guiding others and leading teams, a leader eventually emerges from the Toastmasters program.

I had seen a Toastmasters flyer on the bulletin board at work one day. I had always wanted to get involved with Toastmasters, and here was my chance.

So, I took a deep breath, found my courage and attended the first Toastmasters meeting in Restaurant Row. I found out it was a new club, and the sponsors were trying to recruit people to attend meetings. Some of the sponsors were Caroline Kunitake, Teri Fabry, and Jason Baguio. They were nice people—hospitable, compassionate, energetic, and knowledgeable.

I was so interested in what I saw and heard at the first meeting that I immediately signed up to do my "Ice Breaker" speech for the next meeting, which would occur two weeks later.

My first speech "Leaving for a Better Life" was spoken in front of ten new members, as well as Kunitake, Fabry, and Baguio. I was so scared. My heart was beating really fast. I was perspiring, and my hands were shaking. I was so worried about what my new friends would think of me afterwards. But I couldn't dwell on any of that. I had committed to giving a speech, so I stood up in front of the room.

I said my speech in record time, in less than six minutes. I was relieved after I finished.

Caroline came up to me as the meeting was coming to a close and encouraged me to dream big. She said I could do whatever I set my heart to.

My life changed from that point on. I have been a loyal Toastmasters member ever since.

Falling Perfectly Without Trying

During those early meeting days of Toastmasters, I was faced with another huge challenge. It all started when I met with my insurance agent. He encouraged me to have a mammogram. The agency was doing preventive care screenings and giving a benefit of $100 to all women.

Having an extra $100 sounded good to me. Being a single mom, I could use that extra cash for food and utility bills.

I visited the Women's Health Center at the Queen's Medical Center a few days later and had a mammogram. The very next day a nurse called to tell me I needed to get another mammogram as soon as possible, as well as an ultrasound.

What? That was unexpected.

So many things went through my mind that day, including *did I have cancer?* And *what if I died from cancer and left my children motherless*? My mom had gone through cancer treatments a few years earlier, and I was well aware of how her treatment had gone.

It took a while to learn the exact diagnosis, because my internal medicine doctor was on vacation. I had to wait until my doctor came back. As a result, for a couple of weeks I was on an emotional roller coaster ride.

At the end of July 2015, I met with my internal medicine doctor, and he told me that I had the beginning signs of cancer. He referred me to a cancer surgeon, who confirmed the cancer and said it was in the early stages.

I had to have more tests done and see more specialists.

At the same time, I was attending Toastmaster meetings and events. I made appearances at some of the events to talk about domestic abuse, including explaining what it was like to live in a homeless shelter.

I was still writing my memoir and going to work every day. Besides all that, I had a mental illness. It still affects me daily. I believe it started as a result of the abuse I endured. I used to be scared to tell anyone about it, because there is so much negativity surrounding mental illness, especially in the media. Many stories regard people with mental illness as those who do harmful things to other people. As a result, I rarely told people that I'm bi-polar.

A few years ago, I asked my doctor questions about bi-polar issues. He confirmed that I will have the illness for the rest of my life. However, what I didn't realize at the time is that it's important to do your own research on an illness. I was too scared and embarrassed for so long to even admit to myself that I had a psychiatric illness. As a result, I didn't take care of myself like I should have.

I began searching for answers, a cure, and most of all help in early 2017. I needed guidance, but I also needed to become more knowledgeable about living with bipolar disorder so I could better cope with life on a daily basis. Luckily, I was directed to the right group of people, who knew how to help me to understand.

Bipolar disorder is a mental illness that makes an individual experience mania, as well as depression. The depression may include many different symptoms. I experienced the symptoms of social withdrawal, recurring thoughts of death, being in a depressed mood, extreme fatigue, and occasionally I had a loss of interest in things. While the symptoms may cause impairment, they can sometimes last two weeks or more in an episode.

I've also learned to live with mania symptoms. Mania also causes impairment and made me feel abnormally impulsive. My mood swings can be difficult to deal with, sometimes happy, irrational, hyperactive, or angry at different occasions. These feelings can last for a week and may be so severe that I may need to be treated at a hospital.

Some of the other symptoms that others with bipolar feel are having feelings that make them think they have special powers or superiority. They may talk too much or too fast, having racing thoughts, an increase in goal-directed behavior, insomnia, or have extreme self-esteem and euphoria, seeking things that give them pleasure without regard for the consequences. Mania can be dangerous if not treated correctly.

Examples of what mania did to me includes going on a shopping spree when I really didn't have money to spare and staying up all night without feeling the need to sleep.

There are two types of treatment that is used to help people who have been diagnosed with bipolar. One of the treatments includes taking medication, which a psychiatrist will prescribe to the individual.

Another type of treatment is psychotherapy. In order for them to understand the symptoms they experience, they need to learn effective coping skills.

One of the most crucial things I learned from the day treatment center is that suicide is much more common to people who have bipolar compared to people who have been diagnosed with depression. Individuals with bipolar may feel hopeless and experience severe symptoms. That's when the thought of suicide enters their thoughts.

I feel honored to have had the opportunity to attend the outpatient day treatment center three times a week for two and a half months. I have learned so much and met so many wonderful and supportive counselors and patients there. By attending the classes at the treatment center, I had my questions answered, received a great deal of help and support, and didn't feel like an outcast. The classes saved my life.

Despite having bipolar, I managed to walk away from an abusive spouse with my two children to seek a better life for all of us. I know my goals and dreams can overcome all the challenges and obstacles I've gone through, even though it has taken three decades to reach this pinnacle point of my life.

I've learned that life is too short to never ask for help on the important things. I've learned to always remember and believe in your past. Only you know what has happened in your past. No one can take what you have accomplished away from you. You own it, as well as all of your dreams and goals. Those things will help you to overcome all your challenges and obstacles that come your way.

Chapter One

Reminiscing

It was a warm, sunny day in February of 2015 when I walked to my job in Honolulu at the daily newspaper, a soda in one hand, the daily paper in another. As I sat behind my desk in my office chair, I heard my co-workers discussing a breaking news story.

"A mother and her two children were stabbed in their home this morning," Zoe said. "Did you hear about it, Jenny?"

"Oh my goodness!" I replied. "No, I haven't heard." The thought of that poor woman and her children being stabbed cut me to the core. My heart broke for them.

"Such horrible news to start the week," Suzie said.

As they continued to talk about the story, I visited the newspaper's website. Someone had written an article about a twenty-eight-year-old mother, six-year-old boy and eight-year-old girl who had been stabbed multiple times in their Kalihi home. A man had been arrested, and the police believed the suspect knew the family.

The story immediately brought back horrible

memories of the pain and violence that I had faced years ago while living in Vallejo, California with my six-year-old son, five-year-old daughter, and my former husband. It was such a long time ago, but it still hurt.

As I read more of the breaking news article, old memories reeled through my mind. It didn't start when the violence began with my former husband. Rather, the memories went all the way back to my childhood.

I was born at the Queen's Medical Center in Honolulu, raised in Honouliuli, and I later moved to 'Ewa Plantation, also known as Fernandez Village, near the graveyard on Fort Weaver Road. Both my parents were born on O'ahu Island; my dad was raised in Kahuku, which is 35 miles outside of Honolulu and my mom grew up in 'Ewa Plantation, a mere 21 miles from Honolulu.

I'm the oldest child in our family and have four sisters. My dad worked at Foodland, while my mom was a homemaker. Money was tight, but we managed to live on my father's paychecks. Food was scarce. Sometimes, my parents didn't eat so my siblings and I wouldn't go hungry.

On days when we had a little extra, Mom would broil a whole steak or bake a whole chicken for dinner, and we would all eat. At the time, I thought it was a lot. As I got older, I realized I had no idea that my family barely ate enough food while I was young.

As for clothing, we received many hand-me-downs from our cousins on the island. Mom could sew, and as a result, we all had the same kind of outfits made from the same material. This was great for my parents. If we ever got lost in a store or a park, my parents would be able to spot us from afar.

While I grew up in Fernandez Village, my mom's father lived with us and worked in the sugarcane fields. I used to wake up when Grandfather readied himself for work in the morning around 5 AM. He ate soft-boiled eggs with toast before he went to work in his tan-colored clothing and large brim hat.

As he walked out, the old wooden door squeaking shut, I heard a pickup truck stop in front of the house. A few other men were in the truck as well, talking to one another in Filipino. The truck would bring them to the cane fields where they would work all day in the blazing sun.

It was fun growing up in such a big family. One of the things we did on the plantation is watch all the Tournahaulers trucks, which is a 14-foot-tall, 84-foot-long sugar cane truck. The truck carries tons and tons of sugar cane to the mill, where it changes the cane to sugar. In 'Ewa, we would see those gigantic-sized trucks on the way to 'Ewa Elementary School.

My siblings and I played a lot together, and we had many friends on the plantation. We would play at the playground, which had a sliding board, three huge swings, and a see-saw, also known as teeter-totter.

One of the best memories was going to Pakay, a store (in a garage) about two blocks away from where we lived. Lookfun, Pakay's owner, had an IOU book. Grandpa would pick what he wanted, and Lookfun would write it down in the book.

Grandpa paid Lookfun when he received his check.

If we went to the Pakay store with Grandpa, he'd spoil us, buying candy and sodas.

One time, Grandpa bought a couple of live Samoan crabs from Lookfun. He dropped them in a large bucket and covered it with a heavy lid. When we got home, he put the bucket on the grass and went into the house.

While he was gone, the crabs crawled out of the bucket, out onto the sidewalk, and then under our house, which was on stilts.

My sisters and I thought it was hilarious, especially when Grandpa tried to look for the crabs under the house. He didn't find them, so we couldn't have them for dinner that evening.

"Hmm, crab salad for lunch sounds good," I said to my co-worker, opening my email and forgetting my fond memories of Grandpa.

***

Later than night, after I got home and dinner was put away, I sat in my chair and reminisced about my childhood.

My siblings and I attended 'Ewa Elementary School, where a statue of Abraham Lincoln graced the front of the school. Every year on February 12, the school celebrated Lincoln's birthday. It was a big event with a long program. It was a big thing to us kids to have a statue of a former president adorned with beautiful colorful leis on his birthday.

I laughed out loud at the sight my mind conjured and wondered if the school still had a similar celebration.

Falling Perfectly Without Trying

When I was eight years old, I went to Pakay with Grandpa, and we bought soda for the family. I helped carry the soda home and into the kitchen, entering from the back door.

I called for Mom, who was in her bedroom with my baby sister, Deanna. She emerged without the baby and walked through the living room, approaching the spot in the kitchen where I stood.

She opened the refrigerator door, about to help me put the cans inside, but then she panicked as she looked toward her bedroom.

She told me to go outside, then frantically ran into the living room toward her bedroom. I rushed out the back door as people ran into the house with a garden water hose bursting with water and it spilling everywhere.

Our house was on fire, and smoke poured into the living room from the bedroom.

My siblings ran to the front of the house, where they saw Mom handing my young baby sister to a basketball player who came over to help. They had been on their way to Pakay when they ran back to the house because they could hear Mom yelling for Grandpa for help. Then, they saw Mom climb out the window.

It was such a chaotic day, with Mom crying and running to make sure we were all safe.

Grandpa tried to help with the water hose. People from all over the plantation housing came to help out. Many of the men rushed into the house and carried out our belongings, leaving it on the grass in our yard. The neighborhood ladies tried to comfort my siblings and I as we all looked at our burning house with disbelief.

We all wondered the same thing. How did the fire start?

Minutes went by before the plantation firefighters arrived to douse out the remaining fire, which had slowly stopped burning.

Dad came home from work and hugged Mom, while my siblings and I stood close to our neighbor's house, crying and wondering where we would live now.

A few hours passed by and things calmed down. Mom stopped crying and looked over the items that were saved from the fire: tables, a sewing machine, beddings, sofa, a stereo, chairs, and some clothing. Grandpa thanked all of our neighbors for helping with the fire. The fire fighters continued to smother the burnt items and wood floors with water until it was completely out. The fire fighter captain told my parents that he believed the fire started due to faulty electrical wiring.

As the sun began to go down and night came, we gathered together in our neighbor's house. Mom, Dad, Grandpa, my sisters and I were still in shock. Our neighbor made dinner to comfort us.

Dad used our neighbor's phone to call Aunty Eva, his older sister. He hoped she would let us stay at her home for a little while. After he told her what happened, she immediately said yes, please come.

Dad called us together, and we all got into his green station wagon. Then he drove us to Aunty Eva's house in Wahiawa and stayed with her family until we were able to get another house in 'Ewa Plantation.

The tears rolled down my face as I remembered the ride to Eva's house with little more than the clothes on our backs, mother's handbag, a blanket as well as some toys, which the neighborhood children willingly gave us. We practically didn't have anything. Most of our belongings, clothes, toys, furniture and school supplies burned in the fire.

***

A month later, we moved into a larger plantation house in Tenney Village, which was about 2 miles from our house that burned down. It had a huge mango tree in the back yard and a small wooden building next to the mango tree, which housed the washer. In the front yard, there was a plumeria tree. My sisters and I were happy at how big our new yard was because we had so much more space to play. Dad bought a gym set for us, which included swings and a sliding board.

One of the things my sisters and I liked about the location of our new home was that it was across from a concrete yard that was owned by 'Ewa Plantation. The concrete yard was empty and no one worked there on a daily basis. As a result, we always played with the concrete, which was scattered over a couple of blocks. Hide-N-Seek was our favorite game to play in the concrete yard, because we could hide between the concrete blocks without getting hurt.

I approached my sisters one day about what they thought of Mom and Dad having another baby, and they all thought it was a good idea. We went to them to ask, but Mom told us it would require a lot of hard work, asking if we would be willing to help out.

"Of course," I said. "We would be happy to help as much as we possibly can."

Months later, Mom got pregnant and gave birth to our brother, Dean. We were so elated to have a new addition to our family.

I glanced up at a picture of my family on the wall, my brother in the middle of us girls. We had doted on him so much as a baby.

***

The next morning, I went to work but the thoughts of when I was in school kept flooding my mind.

The years had passed, and I started attending Ilima Intermediate School. My parents submitted an application to get a house in a new subdivision called 'Ewa Estates. Afterwards, they made a promise to God that if they got the house, they would start going to church as a family.

After much anticipation and many prayers, my parents were among the applicants chosen. They gathered us together nearly every day to visit the site where our house would be built. We got to see the house built from the two by fours, and we were so excited to watch the progress.

Our new house had four bedrooms, two bathrooms, a living room and a connected dining room, and a big yard. To us, the house would be brand-new.

When it was finished, we moved in. However, Grandpa opted to stay in the plantation house in Tenney Village. He was more comfortable there.

Falling Perfectly Without Trying

As a family, we all pitched in to plant grass in our yard. First, we had to soften the dirt since there were so many rocks and stones in the yard. Then, we planted the grass and some plant seeds, which turned into beautiful roses and orchids. After a few months, the yard looked beautiful!

A year passed before my sister, Annabelle, reminded my parents about their promise to God if we got the house.

"We've been here a year already, and we still aren't going to church," Annabelle said. "You promised God that if we got this house, we would attend church as a family."

That weekend, we found a church Mom liked, and went to service as a family. After going a couple of times to Sunday services at Our Lady of Perpetual Help Church, Father Hector asked Dad to play music for mass, a request Dad couldn't refuse.

Dad was honored to do so, and he encouraged my sisters to play the guitar and organ so they could contribute their talents to the family church choir.

Mom also became heavily involved with the church. She would sweep the floors, wipe down the pews, or fix the church liturgical books on the shelves behind the pews. Several times, she bought flowers and arranged them on the altar.

While our family became active church participants, my siblings and I got involved with various church clubs and retreats. It was in one of these groups that I met my future husband, Miguel. He and his family were active in the church activities. I got to know

Miguel and hung out with him and his friends often.

PAX was a group for the teens that attended the church. It wasn't too big, and we met once a week. As a result, the members were a close-knit circle of friends who were more like a support group for each other. We hung out with each other at school and went on weekend retreats together as well.

Growing up in O'ahu had its good times and bad times. Since I was the oldest child, my parents were much stricter on me. I couldn't date boys or go to school dances. I was told I couldn't pierce my ears until I was sixteen, and by the time I reached that age, I was too frightened to do so. My parents constantly reminded me that I had to be a good example for my siblings.

There was a church group for teens that my sisters and I got involved in. It was called Filipino Catholic Club for Teens. Most of the churches on the island had an FCC for teens as well as for adults, so we had huge events and fundraisers.

Every year, the club had a candy fundraiser. If a church sold the most candies, they would choose a teen girl from their church to represent their FCC club in a gala pageant where the teen would dress in a traditional Filipino dress and tiara.

One year later, our FCC club sold the most candies, and I was chosen as the queen (to represent our church at the gala event. I went to The Big Island of Hawai'i with all the different Catholic Churches, who had a Filipino club at their church. It was a very prestigious gala event and being part of the gala pageant made it even more special. I was honored to be chosen by my own (Our Lady of Perpetual Help) FCC club members and to represent our church on the Big Island of Hawai'i.

As I got older, I became involved with Search, a spiritual weekend for youths between the ages of thirteen and twenty-two who belonged to Catholic churches around the island. It was a well-organized church function that included team members who met weekly before each Search retreat. I tried to be part of the team for a while, but I was much too shy.

My sisters and I were brought up so religiously that two of my sisters, Annabelle and Bertha, entered a convent while still in high school. It was a joyous, wonderful occasion to have two sisters entering a religious order. It was also sad because they would be stationed in Boston. We wouldn't see them for years when we were young.

Bertha eventually came home from the convent and lived at Mom's house for a couple of years. However, Annabelle stayed in the convent and served God for many years.

I thought about calling Annabelle that night to check on her. It'd been a while since we last spoke.

***

My parents encouraged us to enjoy quiet activities. One of the things that my sisters and I loved to do was read. We would go to the library and borrow as many books as we could carry home. My favorites were *Pippi Longstocking*, *Charlotte's Web*, science fiction books, and crime or mystery novels.

Annabelle loved to read so much that she kept a set of books in our bedroom and made sure they were in order. Her favorites were *Funk & Wagnalls New World Encyclopedia*, books written by Jacques Cousteau and the *Science Encyclopedia*.

I continued to be a reader as I attended James Campbell High School located in 'Ewa Beach. I wasn't a popular student. I didn't join a lot of clubs, although I did participate in a Medical Careers club for a while. I had many friends from different backgrounds, and many of our church friends attended Campbell.

Throughout my four years at Campbell, I did well academically but I was a very shy, quiet young woman. I would spend hours and hours on my homework and studying for tests and exams.

While I was in high School at Campbell, Miguel became good friends to my sisters, and I considered him a brother. I looked up to him. I thought he was wise beyond his years and smart, and I was so happy he was part of my life. I didn't ever question his motives.

My sisters, friends, Miguel, and I would cut class on occasion and hang out at the beach in the Nanakuli and Waianae area. Before Miguel's graduation, we drove around the island in two cars that belonged to other church members. We went to the North Shore, Waimea Bay, Kaneohe, as well as stopped at the Honolulu Zoo in Waikiki. We had so much fun!

Miguel and some of our church friends (from Our Lady of Perpetual Help Church in Ewa Beach) graduated from Campbell that year. It was so sad to see everyone leaving school. To make matters worse, a week later, Miguel enlisted in the US Army Airborne Rangers. His training would be in Fort Bragg, NC. Before he left, Miguel promised me that he would continue to call whenever possible and write to me. His promises seemed sincere, and we tearfully said goodbye to each other at the airport.

After his basic training ended, we stayed in touch. I wrote him letters every week telling him of all the things my sisters and I did to keep busy. Most of the time we just studied and did our homework, and there were events at church (OLPH) that took place every week. Some of the events were geared to high school teenagers.

When high school graduation came up the following year, with over 500 students in my senior class, I was ranked in the top 10. It made my parents proud. All those nights of staying up past midnight to do homework and not going to school functions had paid off. Graduation day was held at the high school campus. I was so happy and proud that day to walk with my class.

After graduation, I didn't pursue higher education, because Mom had always told us, "You don't need a college degree to go to work. You can work from the bottom and climb your way up."

That summer, I worked for a clothing store in downtown Honolulu. I enjoyed working there. I'd buy many outfits for my sisters and I.

In the autumn, I needed a change from the retail world. I went to work as a mailroom clerk at a bank in downtown, and then I transferred to their credit department.

While at the bank, my relationship with Miguel bloomed. At first, it was the brother/sister relationship we had in high school. I looked up to him and felt I needed someone I could trust for advice. Miguel was just the right person to fill that position. It felt nice being like a sister to him. He would treat me so well.

Miguel had a girlfriend who was also from Hawai'i. However, it wasn't working out between them. As a result, Miguel called it off and they broke up.

In high school, I didn't interact with anyone unless they were from the church. My parents didn't want my sisters and I to get romantically involved with any young men while we were in high school.

As a result, the friendship I had with Miguel was the only serious relationship I had. While he was in the Army, Miguel and I continued to correspond with each other through mail and telephone calls. As the months went by, my feelings for Miguel grew, and I began to look at him a different way. But he wasn't sure about having a relationship with me.

He had an opportunity to come home on leave for a few days, and during that time we realized we cared for each other deeply. We made a commitment to stay faithful to each other while maintaining a long-distance relationship.

Miguel was 5'11" tall. He had black hair in a military-cut style, brown eyes, and muscular. Whenever I was with him, he stood tall, straight, and proud. He looked especially handsome in his uniform.

I admired the qualities he had. He was compassionate,

trusting, but down-to-earth and mellow. He was passionate about his religious beliefs, and being in the military meant he was stable and financially secure to me.

Because he served as an Airborne Ranger, he traveled to many different states, and had a tour in Korea. Whenever he traveled, he lavished me with gifts, including blankets, clothing, jackets, and jewelry. His generosity and kindness overwhelmed me.

After a few years of being stationed at Fort Bragg, he transferred to Schofield Barracks on O'ahu to be closer to me. We spent all our free time together. We went to parties, different island events, church activities, or just hung out with the family at the beach.

After work one day, Miguel asked me if I would like to spend a weekend in Waikiki.

"Yeah, that sounds like fun," I said, "but I should ask my parents first."

Worried as I was, I thought my parents would immediately disagree to the weekend in Waikiki. I went home that night and asked them.

They agreed to let me go, but made me promise that Miguel and I would have separate hotel rooms for the weekend. As a result, Miguel made reservations for two separate hotel rooms for the weekend.

On Friday night, we had dinner at a steak and seafood restaurant located in the hotel.

"Wow, it's beautiful, Miguel," I said. "We can see Waikiki beach and the sunset from our table. I can't believe that we are really here."

"I'm glad you like it, Jenny," Miguel said. "I always wanted to bring you here."

Jenny Duhaylonsod Delos Santos

Being from 'Ewa Beach, I had never been in a restaurant as beautiful as that one, nor did I ever have much of a chance to go to Waikiki before. I was swept away by the experience.

Looking at the menu, I was appalled by the prices. "Miguel, it's so expensive," I said. "Maybe we should go somewhere else."

"No," Miguel said firmly. "Let's stay here for dinner. You can order whatever you want."

I was reluctant to do so, but to please him I chose roasted Jidori chicken. It was a much lower cost compared to all the steaks and seafood.

As we waited for our dinner, we relaxed and listened to a small musical group playing in the corner of the restaurant.

"It's so breathtaking, Miguel," I exclaimed. "I will always remember this moment."

Looking towards me he smiled and said, "I'm glad you like this restaurant."

The waitress brought our choices to us.

"The food is delicious," I said. "I'm glad I chose the roasted chicken."

Miguel agreed, "Yeah, this prime New York steak is awesome!"

After we ate, Miguel asked me, "Would you like to go on the lanai and watch the waves come up to the beach?"

I immediately perked up. "That would be so romantic."

As the night wore on, we walked around the hotel and saw a bar and a nightstand where they sold flowers.

Falling Perfectly Without Trying

Miguel surprised me by buying three beautiful red roses while I went to the restroom.

"The bouquet is so beautiful, Miguel," I said. "Thank you. I will remember this night forever."

The rest of the weekend was just as wonderful. We spent hours at the Honolulu Zoo, the Waikiki Aquarium, the International Market Place and relaxed on the beach near the hotel. When we got back to my house late Sunday night, I didn't want the weekend to end. I kept hugging him while I sat next to him in my family's house garage.

Miguel was my first real boyfriend. I couldn't think straight when I was around him. I was so head-over-heels in love with him. I didn't realize I was too naïve to have such a serious relationship.

Most of the time, we kissed and hugged one other whenever we were together. However, we had so much passion for each other that I soon lost my virginity. Four months went by, and I realized I was pregnant.

Miguel and I discussed the pregnancy, and he knew he had to ask my parents for my hand in marriage.

My parents agreed. They were overjoyed to have Miguel officially a part of the family. We were so in love, it seemed the natural thing to do.

My grandmother, my mom's mother, who was a seamstress, designed my wedding dress. I had a maid of honor and a flower girl—two of my sisters. Our families wanted a small reception after the marriage ceremony.

Four months later, Miguel and I got married at our church. It was a very "hush-hush" experience since I was pregnant.

Reverend Carter, an associate pastor of the church, as well as a wonderful mentor and friend to Miguel and I, performed the marriage ceremony. After the ceremony, we had a small party in front of my family's home in 'Ewa Beach. We had lots of food, and Miguel's parents prepared a whole roasted pig a "lechon" for the joyous occasion.

A lot of the guests that attended the celebration were from our parish, which we thought was surprising. Our relatives and extended family also came to the party, and everyone had a lot of fun.

Life wasn't easy after we were married. We lived with Miguel's family in Mililani until I gave birth to our son in September.

The night our son, Michael, was born was so scary for me. It was not a good experience. It was still one month before my due date and I was still working at the bank. I went home late from work that evening. I caught the Bus to get home from work.

When I reached the Bus stop in Mililani, I was so tired and very uncomfortable. I was in my eighth month of pregnancy. After a few minutes, Miguel came from the U.S. Army base in Wahiawa to pick me up in his green hot rod car, which he had fixed so that it would go really fast. I was happy he came, and we went home to his family's house.

I changed my work clothes into pajamas and went to sleep. At approximately 1 AM, my water broke, and I got up.

I saw blood all over the blankets under me. I was so

scared. I thought I had lost our baby.

I woke up Miguel, who was sleeping next to me. He stirred with a grumpy sound.

He got up and was surprised to see so much blood on the bed. He ran to get his mother, and they helped me out of bed and wiped me down with clean towels.

Miguel drove me to Tripler Army Medical Center. At the hospital, several nurses helped me change my clothes and put me in a wheeled bed. I could feel the baby coming.

I had the urge to push, and the nurses said I was dilated to 10 centimeters already. Realizing the baby was coming, they pushed me into the Surgery Room. It was a fast labor. I was happy to meet our baby boy. He was physically fine at 4 pounds, 11 ounces. I stayed in the hospital with Michael for a few days before we were allowed to go home. The nurses and doctor were worried I might get an infection afterwards, but I didn't.

As the months went by, my in-laws, my family and I enjoyed taking care of Michael, especially since he was the first grandchild on both sides. Thankfully, I had taken care of my cousin's babies many times, so I knew what to do to take care of a baby.

My mother-in-law insisted everything be done her way, and I tried really hard to obey her. However, there were times I wouldn't, and we would get into heated arguments.

When Miguel came home from work at the army base in Wahiawa, he would get mad at me. He insisted that I take care of Michael and do any chores the way his mother wanted. I tried, but I wasn't able to live up to her standards. My relationship with my mother-in-law started to suffer.

It was difficult living there for me. I felt like I had to obey Miguel for every single thing he asked for, too. One of the hardest things I had to do was succumb to my husband's wishes whenever he wanted to have sex. That started just three weeks after I delivered Michael. I told Miguel I didn't want to, that I wasn't ready, but he insisted.

His requests were frequent, and it was difficult to turn him away. As a result, I got pregnant again not long after.

By the time I was in my third trimester, I was going to regular check-ups. My doctor realized that my womb was infected. I was so scared and worried. I thought my baby wasn't going to survive. I was just seven months pregnant.

At first, my doctor moved me into the labor room for a few hours. There, they did tests and realized the baby was dying. They had to do an emergency surgery in order for both me and the baby to survive.

They put me to sleep by giving me anesthesia, telling me that everything would be fine when I woke up.

When I finally did wake up, I was in the Intensive Care Unit with seven IVs in me, which had been put in various parts of my body—my arms, legs, feet, and even my neck. One of the IVs was a blood transfusion. The doctors explained that I was dying and needed more blood to replace the amount I had lost during surgery. Our daughter, who we named Remie, was three pounds, two ounces, and thankfully, a fighter.

Falling Perfectly Without Trying

She needed a lot of help to survive the ordeal and the infection.

I was in ICU for a couple of days. I left the hospital on the eighth day, but our daughter was in the nursery's ICU for two long months.

Chapter Two
Torn Down

It was September, and Miguel's brother, Wayne, had started his 12th year of school at Mililani High School. Besides being an A student, Wayne played for the school's football team as a lineman.

During the second weekend after school had started, Mililani High School would play the homecoming game on campus, a mile from where Miguel, Michael, Remie, and I lived with Miguel's family.

That Friday afternoon, when Miguel's father, Chester, got home from work, the whole family decided to go to the football game.

I was sitting on our queen-sized bed in our bedroom. Michael was lying down in the yellow playpen that stood a few inches from the bedroom door. Next to the playpen was a wood crib for Remie. She was still tiny and petite for her age.

As I held Remie on the big bed and fed her with a baby bottle, Miguel walked into the bedroom with a determined look on his face.

"I'm going with Mom, Dad, and my brothers to the football game tonight to watch Wayne play," he said.

Falling Perfectly Without Trying

"No, you can't go," I said. "Who's going to help me watch the babies?"

Since we had brought Remie home from the hospital a month and a half ago, I never stayed alone with both babies. I usually had one of Miguel's family members stay with me. As a result, I was very unsure of myself of being able to care for Michael and Remie on my own.

Miguel stood a few feet away from me and Remie and leaned forward, yelling loudly, "I'm going to the football game no matter what you say, you good-for-nothing, worthless slut."

The baby stirred in my arms and Michael looked up at his dad with a look of terror.

Miguel's mother came to the door, looking worried. "Miguel, you'll have to stay home and help Jenny with the children."

Miguel walked over to the doorway. "Go then, Mom." He quietly closed the door while I put the sleeping Remie into her crib.

He turned and stepped closer to me. He put his face a few inches from my left ear and yelled into it. "You're a sickening whore and fat and ugly. You're gonna get it!"

A temper tantrum had started. Miguel stomped around to his side of the bed, flopped down unto it, and turned his whole body to face the door. Pouting.

I could hear the rest of the family go through the front door of the house and drive away in their black car.

Ten minutes later, Michael started to cry in his

playpen and Remie stirred from her sleep.

I immediately hurried to the kitchen to get two bottles of milk from the refrigerator and went back to our bedroom.

I gave Michael one of the bottles, and picked up Remie. I carried her to the far side of the bed, opposite of Miguel's. While I tried to feed the baby, Michael started to cry again.

Miguel got up from the bed and stood next to Michael, who was sitting in his playpen.

"You better shut up, Michael!" Miguel yelled. "You're such a spoiled rotten kid. Shut up! Shut up now."

Michael was frightened and continued to cry. I held Remie tightly in my arms. I was so scared.

Suddenly, Miguel slapped Michael on the face and didn't stop.

I was speechless, I was so shocked by his behavior. I couldn't move. I was paralyzed. This wasn't the Miguel I had grown to love. After he finally stopped slapping Michael, Miguel opened the bedroom door, walked out, and slammed the door shut.

I put Remie in the crib and lay her down. Then I went to comfort Michael, who was still crying and sniffling.

His face was extremely bruised. It made my heart ache. I carried him to the bed and tried to soothe him. I cuddled my toddler for a long time, tears rolling down my face.

I let Michael lay on our bed until he fell asleep. Remie continued to sleep in her crib. So many things were going through my mind. I was afraid that Miguel would come back into the bedroom and explode again. I was twenty-two-years old and didn't know what to do. I was so scared for the well-being of my children and myself.

My mind was filled with so much fear and despair as I waited for Miguel's family to come home. An hour and half later, I heard the family's car drive into the garage. I was so relieved.

I lay Michael on the bed, placing pillows around him so he wouldn't roll off it, then walked to the bedroom door and toward the front door. As I opened it, I saw Miguel's Mom and Dad.

I blurted out, "Miguel hit Michael."

Miguel's mom searched my face. "What do you mean? Where's Michael now?"

"Inside. On my bed."

Mom and Dad followed me into the bedroom where Michael lay asleep on the queen-sized bed. His cheeks were already swollen and bruised.

"Why did Miguel do that, Jenny?" Patricia cried out. "Michael is just a baby."

"Miguel wanted to go to the game," I explained. "Because he couldn't, this is what happened. We should bring Michael to the hospital, make sure no bones are broken."

"No," she said. "Miguel can get into big trouble. We'll take care of the baby ourselves."

I couldn't believe what I was hearing. They wouldn't help me bring my baby to the emergency room, and I didn't know how to drive so I couldn't take him myself.

"We cannot let anyone see Michael until the swelling

goes down, and Jenny, you cannot go outside with the children," Patricia said.

I reluctantly agreed, but I was so lost...so heartbroken...and so scared.

Three days later, Miguel was deployed to Korea. As a result, I begged my in-laws to let me visit my parents in 'Ewa Beach. At first, they didn't think it was a good idea and didn't allow it. But after asking Patricia over and over the same question, she let us go, and my parents came to pick up the children and I.

When my parents saw Michael, they were shocked. Even hours later, Miguel's handprints were noticeable on the baby's face. My entire family were stunned to learn that Miguel's parents didn't bring us to the emergency room.

"If Miguel ever hits the children or you, Jenny, please call us right away," Mom said. "I'm very upset that Michael wasn't brought to the hospital."

That was the first violent episode. We stayed with my parents and siblings in 'Ewa Beach for over a month while Michael healed.

Miguel came home from Korea, and without an apology or talking about what he did, we went on as if nothing had happened to Michael. The kids and I returned to his family home in Mililani.

As the months went by, life became a roller coaster ride. Because Miguel and I lived with his family, I interacted with Patricia every day. There were times when I would say something to Patricia and she would get easily offended. Other times, she acted as if she hadn't heard me. It was frustrating.

Falling Perfectly Without Trying

Patricia insisted that I use her care techniques. I didn't believe placing a dry cloth diaper on my children's back would prevent them from getting sick. I expressed my reasons to her on how I felt. Patricia got offended and suddenly become physically sick.

When Miguel found out what happened, he got furious at me. He threatened me by saying he would throw the children and me out of the house, and we would become homeless.

I panicked and begged my mother-in-law for forgiveness. It took all night for Patricia to feel better. Miguel continued to intimidate me until the next morning.

It got worse every day. I couldn't believe the nightmare I was living in. Miguel controlled everything that I did, where I went and whom I saw. He forced me to beg him or others for money when I needed to purchase things and told me to quit my job.

I was isolated and alone. The only time I was ever happy was when I was with my children. I spent all my time with Miguel's parents and brothers after they came home from their jobs or from being at school.

One day, Miguel got into an argument with his mom and the relationship between his father and brothers were strained. As a result, we spent a great deal of time outside of the house. During the weekends, we went to the beach, ate dinner at a fast food restaurant with the kids or visited with Miguel's friends.

The following year, Miguel received transfer papers to Fort Lewis, Washington. With the help of the US Army, our belongings were boxed up and shipped to the army base. Miguel was told he would be stationed there for two years.

Miguel had bought a brand-new Quantum station wagon. It was a beautiful car, but I had little experience behind the wheel. It frightened me whenever I had to drive it.

If Miguel was in the car, he always raised his voice and yelled at me whenever I drove. I think he did it because it was a new car, and he didn't want anything to happen to it. He seemed to care more for the car than me some days.

Miguel went ahead of us to look for an apartment in Tacoma, Washington, because he was told his family couldn't live on base right away. After Miguel left, Michael, Remie, and I went to live with my family in 'Ewa Beach.

I enjoyed being back home. I was able to relax and not worry about my children's safety. Our life was great living with Mom, Dad, and my sisters. Everyone got along well with each other and there was no friction.

Many days, my sisters and I would take my children to the mall in Pearl City. We also spent a great deal of time at the church since my family was still very much involved with the clubs, religious classes, and being a part of the Sunday mass. Dad had continued to play his guitar during mass whenever the priest made the request for him to play. My children flourished under so much love and devotion.

***

Falling Perfectly Without Trying

Three months later, three-year-old Michael and two-year-old Remie and I made the long journey to Washington. Our first day with Miguel was somewhat pleasant. He picked us up from the airport and brought us home to our new apartment in Tacoma. After I changed the children and we refreshed ourselves with drinks of water, we set out for a nearby park. The weather was 65 degrees. That was cold for Hawaiian standards. I bundled up the kids in warm clothing while everyone else in the park wore tank tops and shorts. It was so funny!

Although he was stationed in Fort Lewis, Miguel could be sent to other states or a different country at a moment's notice. If that happened, the kids and I would stay in Washington. I realized quickly that I would have to learn how to fend for the children and myself. I would need to drive us all over the city without Miguel.

Two days after I arrived in Washington, Miguel forced me to sit in the driver's seat of our car. As I drove, Miguel yelled at me.

First, I missed a turn onto a ramp off of the freeway. He yelled and screamed at me to find a way to get off the freeway. I found an exit and stopped on the center island between the lanes in the middle of the traffic lights. I turned off the engine and looked at him. "You should drive, Miguel."

However, Miguel didn't move. Instead, he screamed at me.

He got out of the car and marched away to the corner, looking in the other direction from us.

Meanwhile, our two children sat in the back seat

of the station wagon in their car seats crying. I had to get them to safety. The intersection was getting busy and people were staring at us. I got out of the car and begged Miguel to come back. Calm again, we both got back in the car and he told me where to drive.

Living in Washington was very hard. Miguel continued to call me mean names, ridicule me, and make me feel bad about myself. To make matters worse, he wasn't happy to be stationed at Fort Lewis. He didn't care for the people he worked with, either. Michael, Remie, and I didn't like it there because it was dreary and cold all the time compared to Hawai'i.

November 1985 came, and I saw snow for the first time. The children were so excited. As the first snowflakes fell from the sky, I held out a big frying pan outside the living room window, hoping to catch the snow in it. I didn't realize it would just melt as it fell into the frying pan. I laughed out loud and the kids joined me. We thought it was so funny!

Later that day, the children and I walked outside and played in the snow. It was an unforgettable moment watching them touch and play with snow for the very first time. It was a rare day of laughter and fun.

Months went by, and we finally had permission to move on base at Fort Lewis. The house we occupied had two bedrooms, a bathroom, a large living room, kitchen, and a place to wash and dry our clothes. It was quaint but big enough for the four of us. The yard was also very huge.

Living on base had his advantages and disadvantages. Miguel continued to order me around, but he didn't hurt the children. I was forced to do all the chores by myself, including the heavier chores like mowing the yard. It was very difficult, and I went to bed exhausted every day.

A year and a half later, Miguel realized he wanted to get out of the army. We later thought and decided of a plan to move our family to Vallejo, California, where Miguel's aunt, uncle and two cousins lived. The idea of moving closer to relatives sounded very appealing. At least, we wouldn't be entirely alone in California.

While Miguel packed and shipped our belongings to California, he sent the children and I back to Hawai'i for the summer months. We stayed with my parents and siblings in 'Ewa Beach, and I found a summer job in downtown Honolulu so I wouldn't have to depend on Miguel for money.

Every morning I'd catch the Bus and it'd take me all the way into the city where I was a clerk at a credit department in a local bank. I really enjoyed my job duties and getting to know my co-workers. I was getting used to my daily routine, which included not having my husband around. I was no longer the naïve young woman. I knew what Miguel was capable of and wanted to stay clear of him.

During that time, Miguel was discharged from the army and living with his relatives in Vallejo. He spent his hours searching for a job and a place for us to live.

A month went by. Miguel found a job with an armored car company and started saving money in order to afford a place for us to live. Eventually, he found a nice one-bedroom apartment complex in the newer part of Vallejo. There were a few units available to rent there.

However, by that time, Michael, Remie, and I were used to living in Hawai'i. I was happy and didn't want to go back to California.

But Miguel coaxed me into going to visit him without the children. Reluctantly, I traveled to California by myself. While I was with Miguel, he somehow managed to convince me that life would be better for me in California. He promised he wouldn't yell at me anymore and that he would treat me better.

Naturally, I believed him. I agreed to go back to Hawai'i, get the children, and return to California.

I put in my two weeks' notice at my job at the bank and everyone was sad to see me go. A month went by since Miguel had encouraged us to come back and be a family again.

With all our boxes and suit cases, as well as manapuas, pork hash, rice cake and numerous leis all lined up at the United Airlines terminal—at that time, there was no limit to the amount of boxes and suitcases we could bring onto the plane—Michael, Remie, and I tearfully said good-bye to my family and went back to live in California.

It was September. Michael, Remie, and I arrived at the airport in San Francisco, and the children joyously reunited with their father, who they hadn't seen for three months. Miguel took Remie from my arms and carried her to the car, as Michael and I walked beside him. We drove to our new apartment and settled in quickly.

Falling Perfectly Without Trying

During the week, Miguel worked at an armored car company, and I stayed home to care for Remie and Michael, who attended school a few blocks away. I tried to make friends wherever I went, but it was difficult.

We slowly got used to our daily routine. I noticed Miguel was distancing himself from us, including not talking to us when he would come home from work. He seemed to be very irritable and impatient with us. It was like he was in his own world, and he acted as if we weren't there with him.

One day, Miguel came through the front door after coming home from work. He looked tired and grumpy, and in no mood to talk. He strode straight to our bedroom while I set the table for dinner and the children picked up their toys in the living room. When we were ready to eat, we all gathered around the table. The children talked to each other, but Miguel was quiet and ate, with a stern on his face, which silenced me.

After dinner, I cleaned up in the kitchen while the children got ready for bed. Above the counter, there were cupboards that held pots, pans, and dishes and three loaded silver revolvers. Miguel had put them into the cupboard a few nights before.

At 8 PM, Miguel ordered the children to go to sleep. Michael and Remie changed into their pajamas and went to the bathroom to brush their teeth. Later, they both came to me as I stood next to the kitchen sink. They each gave me a hug and said, "Goodnight Mommy! Love you lots!"

I walked with them to their bedroom to cover them up with their warm blankets. I sat on Remie's bed for a few minutes and sang to her, then quietly, I walked into my bedroom and tidied the room. Miguel sat at the kitchen table and watched television.

After an hour passed, he looked in on the children to make sure they were sound asleep. Then he came into the bedroom where I was and told me to come into the living room.

"Jenny, sit down." Miguel pointed to the carpet a few feet away from him. His tone of voice scared me. It was so harsh and mean, but I sat down. It was hard for me to disobey an order, especially if it came from my husband.

After I crossed my leg and sat on the carpet, Miguel asked, "Are you having an affair with Peter?"

Peter was the mailman for our apartment complex and lived in the same neighborhood as we did. I usually talked to him whenever I saw him delivering mail or going home from work. However, Miguel didn't like the idea that I had male friends, particularly Peter. I enjoyed speaking with all of our neighbors, and I considered Peter one of my closest friends.

"No, I'm not having an affair," I pleaded. "We're just friends."

Miguel reached in his pocket. "Look at this," he said, holding up a grocery store receipt. "You were gone for sixty minutes…alone…yesterday. Where were you?"

"I was at the store buying groceries," I said.

"It doesn't take that long to go to the store and buy things. The store is one block away," he said loudly, not seeming to care if the children woke up. "Usually it takes you thirty minutes at the store. Now, where were you yesterday?"

"I was at the store buying cereal and milk for the children's breakfast tomorrow morning." I tried to calmly answer him so the kids wouldn't wake up.

"No, you weren't. You were with Peter. Tell me the truth—you were with him!"

"No, I wasn't!"

"Wait right here."

Miguel got up, walked to the kitchen cupboard and took out one of his guns. I felt chills go up and down my back as he held it, smiled at me, and carried it toward the living room. He sat a few feet away from me and lowered the gun to the carpet.

"Now tell me again, Jenny," Miguel said. "Did you have an affair with Peter?"

"No, I didn't," I said. Tears filled my eyes and rolled down my cheeks. I was so scared.

"You must've had an affair. You're always talking to him."

"Talking to the mailman doesn't mean we're having an affair."

Miguel reached for the gun with his right hand, lifted it and aimed it inches away from my head.

My life seemed to pass before my eyes, and I cried harder. "Please don't, Miguel!" I said. "I didn't do anything wrong."

"If you don't admit that you and Peter had an affair, I will kill you, the children, and the neighbors," he said.

The threats frightened me. I knew he was serious. Tears rolled down my face until I didn't think I could cry anymore. "There isn't any affair going on. How can

I possibly admit to something that never happened?"

Miguel put the revolver on the carpet. "We will sit here until you admit to it."

As the minutes and hours ticked by, I tried my best to keep sitting upright. Then my body leaned sideways and lurched forward.

He violently shook me. "Wake up, you whore! Did you have an affair with Peter?"

"No, I would never do such a thing," I said.

"You good-for-nothing woman. You're such an ugly person. Nobody will love our children, let alone take care of them if you walk out of our marriage. And you can't leave anyway, because the Catholic Church forbids couples from having a divorce. You do remember that?"

"Yes, I know, Miguel. Please let me sleep," I pleaded. "I'm so tired."

"No, you will sit here until you admit your faults," Miguel said. He grabbed hold of the revolver, aiming the barrel at my face. "Or else I will shoot you and the children. You hear?"

"Please don't!" I panicked. "I never had an affair with Peter or anyone else."

Miguel put the gun back on the carpet next to him. He kept me there sitting upright until 2 AM.

"Go sleep already, but don't you dare tell anyone about tonight or else I'm going to use these guns on you and the children. And Jenny, if you leave, I will hunt you down until I find you. Then I will kill you and the children. You hear?"

I wouldn't dare tell the neighbors about what

happened. The fear of Miguel killing our two children and myself was enough to keep me quiet.

"I promise, I won't tell anyone," I said.

With all the uneasiness and anguish inside of me, I trembled as I got up and left the living room. I kissed my children on their cheeks. I hoped they were sound asleep and hadn't heard anything. They would have nightmares if they had heard Miguel's threats. I retreated to the bedroom to get a few hours of much-needed rest and listened as he put the gun back in the cupboard. I never spoke of that night to anyone.

***

A few days later, it rained steadily. After Miguel came home from work, it poured rain even harder. He wasn't in a mood to talk to anyone. Along with the rain and Miguel's mood swings, Remie had a cold. She had been sniffling and coughing all day.

I was worried about Remie. Two months prior, she'd come down with pneumonia. At the time, I didn't know she was so sick. She'd been coughing, sneezing, had a runny nose, and a hard time breathing properly. One day her temperature shot higher, and I asked Miguel to bring us to the doctor. He said he didn't want to pay a doctor's bill and kept the car keys from me.

I carried her to the bus stop and caught the bus to the nearest clinic. The doctor there admitted her to the hospital with acute pneumonia, where she stayed for a week. I was unable to stay with Remie in the hospital, however, we visited her every evening. The nurses stayed with her so that I wouldn't worry.

While Remie wasn't feeling well again, I felt protective over her. I didn't want to have her admitted into the hospital once more.

I rose from my chair and sat by her on the carpet. I tried to comfort her. But she continued to cough, sniffle, and cry. She feared her father. I felt like I was walking on eggshells again when Miguel started banging on the kitchen table.

"Stop crying, Remie!" Miguel yelled.

But she only cried harder.

"If you don't stop," he said, "I'll make you stay outside in the rain."

I tried hard to calm her down and gave her some tissues, but she continued to wail.

After a few minutes, Miguel picked Remie up and carried her in her pajamas to the front door. He opened it, made her stand on the other side of the door and then closed it behind her.

"Are you crazy?" I demanded. "She's sick, and it's raining."

"What do I care?" Miguel said. "She's going to be okay, and she can't go nowhere because it's raining."

"You're nuts!" I was furious. How could he do such a thing. I stormed to the door, flung it open and carried Remie back into the warm apartment.

"She can get pneumonia again," I said.

Luckily, Remie didn't get pneumonia. I couldn't believe Miguel would be so careless and stupid with our child.

Falling Perfectly Without Trying

***

Over the course of two months, Miguel kept me up at night three times a week while he terrorized and threatened me. He often took a gun from the cupboard and put it next to him while he interrogated me, trying to force me to admit that there was an affair going on. I continued to deny any wrongdoing.

I wasn't sure if Miguel would use the guns on us. I wanted to take my children home to O'ahu, but the guilt of leaving my husband trumped his daily terror. I knew the Catholic Church was strict about married couples separating and divorcing, even if there were any signs of abuse going on in the marriage. *But maybe if I personally spoke to a priest,* I thought, *he would give me permission for the children and I to return to O'ahu.*

I decided to meet with a priest from St. Catherine of Siena Catholic Church for counseling while the children were in school one day. I confided in the priest, Father Gary, and tried to explain what was happening at home. After recalling the threats Miguel said to me, I started to cry. I felt like I was walking on eggshells just thinking about it all.

"Please, Father, can my children and I go home to O'ahu?" I asked amid all my sniffles and tears.

"No, the Catholic church will not allow you to leave your husband," Father Gary said. "Why don't you and your husband come in one day so that we can talk about this situation?"

"I don't know," I said. "I'm not sure if Miguel would

want to come in."

"Well, at least try and ask him," Father Gary said. "He may come in if you ask nicely."

In despair, I returned home on the bus. So many things were going through my mind. Foremost, I felt obligated to stay in Vallejo with my husband, even though I feared for my safety. *How would I continue to handle the daily threats and questions? Would it ever stop? What if he did hurt us?* Would anyone even know something tragic had happened?

After a few days of trying to gather the courage, I asked Miguel if he would see the priest with me.

"What for?" Miguel said. "I didn't do anything wrong. Besides, I don't like talking to priests and have them interfering in our lives."

"But Miguel, we need to talk to someone," I said. "What better way to do it than by going to see a priest?"

"No need!"

The next day, he had a change of heart. "Make an appointment for this Saturday, Jenny, and ask my aunt to watch the kids."

Father Gary talked to us about the value of marriage, as well as how important the Catholic Church wanted married couples to stay married despite any problems the married couple may have.

After almost a half hour of Father Gary talking about religion and marriage, he asked Miguel if there was anything important he needed to discuss.

Miguel said everything was fine between us. We had the usual arguments that married couples had. He noted that all marriages are not free from the usual problems.

While he answered Father Gary, Miguel acted so sincere, nothing like the man he acted like when he was at home.

I couldn't believe it. How could Miguel deny any wrongdoing?

Father Gary asked Miguel if he would sit in the church pews so that he could talk to me privately for a while. Miguel told the priest thank you and left for a pew.

"He seems like a fine young man," Father Gary said. "You have to stay with him. Just be nicer to him and things will work out."

I couldn't understand it. Miguel was extremely nice to other people, but to me, it was a different story. It was like I had made up the whole story about the threats he made to me at night when the children were sleeping. Was I hallucinating?

My family was religious, and my two sisters were Catholic nuns. They probably had the same beliefs that Father Gary lived by. How could I leave Miguel now? I felt leaving him would disgrace my family as a "forbidden" act, according to the Catholic Church. I felt like I was all alone, and no one could help me and my two children.

***

One weekend afternoon, Michael and Remie were sitting on their beds in the living room, watching a cartoon on television. Miguel and I were at the kitchen table. I was busy hemming one of Michael's pants, and

Miguel was wiping down one of his silver revolvers with a cloth.

While we were all in our own little worlds, we could hear Peter, the mailman, quietly depositing the mail into the mail boxes right outside our apartment. Miguel was very agitated with Peter being close by and I was feeling scared since the night before he had terrorized and threatened me again.

Miguel looked up and said bluntly, "Go outside and tell him it's over."

"I don't want to," I said.

"Go outside now," Miguel ordered.

Michael and Remie glanced at us with fear in their eyes.

"Nothing is going on between us, Miguel," I cried out.

"Yes, there must be something going on. Go outside, Jenny," Miguel said.

"I won't!"

"Now! Or else I'm going to get the gun and shoot you and the children."

"Please don't do that," I said, now in tears. "Nothing happened between Peter and I. How can you force me to admit to an affair when nothing happened?"

I walked to the front door and felt my legs giving out beneath me, and my small body sank to the floor.

"What's wrong?" Miguel said. "Get up now!"

I didn't move.

Miguel got up from the kitchen table and moved toward me, nudging my body and legs with his foot.

I tried to speak, but what came out spooked Miguel.

Falling Perfectly Without Trying

Miguel tried to make me sit up. My body was limp and my face was turning pale. He couldn't figure out what was wrong, so he picked me up and moved me to the bedroom. There, he put me on the bed. My body was so cold. I tried to speak, but the words didn't make sense.

"It...s...so...c o l d..." I said slowly, unsteadily, in a whisper.

Miguel touched my arms and face to check my temperature, which was icy cold. He got two blankets from the bedroom closet and the children's blankets from the living room. After a few minutes, he realized that I wasn't getting warm enough.

"I'm sorry, Jenny," Miguel said. He sounded worried, realizing I wasn't well.

The children came into the bedroom and started crying.

"What's wrong with Mommy?" Michael said.

"I don't know," Miguel said. "Go to the living room and stay there."

They went unwillingly, distraught and confused, wondering what had happened to me.

Miguel locked the bedroom door, and our children could be heard on the other side, first trying to twist the knob, then banging on it hysterically.

Miguel paced from one end of the bedroom to the other. "I'm so sorry, Jenny." He banged his head against the wall.

I saw everything unfold, but I still couldn't move. I was temporarily paralyzed.

After some time, Miguel opened the door and let the

children into the bedroom to see me.

"Mommy, Mommy, Mommy," Michael and Remie said as they scurried towards me.

I tried to talk to them, but I was still incoherent. So I slept.

I awoke after an hour. I noticed the children sitting on the floor next to the bed. Miguel sat near the closet.

"I love you, Michael and Remie," I said. The children kissed me on my cheek.

"I promise I won't ever do that again," Miguel whispered.

After an hour passed by, I tried to sit up on the bed with my children next to me, quietly playing with their toys. Miguel got up from the kitchen table and came into the bedroom.

"Why don't we go to the grocery store?" he asked. "Maybe we can get something for dinner tonight."

I still wasn't feeling well, but agreed.

Michael and Remie went to get ready as I tried to pull on long pants and a shirt from my drawer. Then I slowly made my way to the living room to check on the children.

"Okay, let's go," Miguel said to all of us.

With my face still puffy and my skin cold, I grabbed my children's hands as we walked out of the house.

Once outside, I felt myself getting warmer, but I still felt so unsure of myself. I wanted to stay in the house for a little while longer, however, like always, it was hard to disobey my husband.

***

Falling Perfectly Without Trying

The next day, Miguel went to work while the kids and I stayed home.

Around noon, Michael, Remie, and I went to visit our neighbor, Charlene. Charlene was originally from O'ahu, but had moved to Vallejo two years ago with her husband, George. I got along well with her, especially since we came from the same hometown.

As soon as she saw me, she knew something was wrong.

"What happened, Jenny?" she asked, suspicious. "You don't look well. Your face is so pale and puffy, and you look tired."

I tried to explain, but couldn't. Tears kept brimming in my eyes. The children played nearby and I tried to smile at Michael when he waved to me. But I couldn't. The fear of being terrorized and interrogated troubled me. I remembered that Miguel had told me not to talk to anyone about it. I didn't explain to her what happened, but Charlene could tell something was wrong by just looking at me.

"You should leave him," Charlene said.

"He said it won't happen again."

"I doubt that." Charlene put her arm around me and led me to a bench to sit down.

That evening, Miguel came home with flowers. He handed the bouquet to me and said, "I'm sorry, Jenny. It'll never happen again." Then he kissed my cheek.

For the next two weeks, Miguel and I were back in our honeymoon phase. He came home with small little gifts of chocolate and flowers three times that first week. He was so sweet and nice to Michael, Remie, and I. He did most all of the chores while I cooked dinner. He stayed with the children and they enjoyed his playfulness. It was as if our violent past of suspicions and threats had never happened. The next week was more of the same behaviors.

***

A few weeks later, on one Sunday morning after church, I talked to Priscilla and Tom, members of the church choir. The couple occasionally talked to the children and I, and on this particular Sunday, I briefly mentioned the marital problems Miguel and I were having.

They asked if they could bring over the Our Lady of Fatima statue to our house and pray the rosary with our family. The statue was a replica of the original statue sculpted in 1947, based on a description by Sr. Lucia, one of the three young children who saw Mother Mary in person in 1917 in Fatima, Portugal. There were a number of replicas based on the original statue, and one of those statues had come to Vallejo.

The rosary is a form of prayer used by members of the Catholic Church. It is a string of beads that is used to count prayers including the Lord's Prayer, the Hail Mary, Glory Be, and Angel of God. When Catholics recited the rosary, sometimes it was specifically for a reason or asking the mother of Jesus, Mary, for help on a personal favor.

While growing up in Hawai'i, we said the rosary often and had multiple statues that went from one

Falling Perfectly Without Trying

church to another. As a result, I welcomed the idea that Priscilla proposed, which was to bring the statue to our apartment.

"Maybe if we pray to Mother Mary, then things will change for the better," Priscilla reasoned. "Do you think your husband would mind if Tom and I came over to your house?"

"He won't mind," I said. "Why don't you visit us on Wednesday evening?"

When the three of us went home after church, I wasn't sure how Miguel would react. I shuffled the kids into their room to play and tested the waters. He seemed to be in good spirits, but I wasn't sure if he would like the idea of visitors. I explained to him that Priscilla and Tom were coming on Wednesday to bring the statue and pray the rosary.

"Maybe it'll bless this house," I told him.

He remained quiet for the rest of the afternoon.

It wasn't until nightfall that he finally said it was okay for Priscilla and Tom to visit.

Wednesday arrived quickly, along with the statue. My family was in complete awe. The statue was beautiful, with white features. Her crown was gold and sparkly, and the statue's robe was white, but sparkled like it had glitter on it.

As we all prayed the rosary, we could smell roses. It was so weird—the rose scent, and it stunned all of us, including Priscilla and Tom. They weren't sure where it had come from.

Before they left, Priscilla promised they would pray for my family.

During the rest of the week, Miguel was extra nice to us. I was so happy that he treated our children and I so nicely. He didn't yell at us or threaten me at all.

***

It had been four weeks since that dreadful day when I had slumped to the floor in fear. I later was told I had a "chemical imbalance," which is sort of like a nervous breakdown. Life had been less stressful since that night, but my nightmare was about to resume again.

Miguel came home from work one day and wasn't in the mood to talk to anyone. Later, after both children were asleep, he commanded me to sit on the floor.

Miguel grabbed a big butcher knife from the utensil drawer and one of his guns from the cupboard. He put them on the floor next to him as he sat down in his recliner.

"Now, tell me that you and Peter are having an affair," he said.

I sat down on the floor, but I couldn't believe it was happening again.

"No, Miguel, nothing happened between Peter and I. If it had happened, I would've told you."

"If you don't admit it, I will use this knife on you. Then, I'll kill myself with the knife."

"No, please don't," I cried. "I promise you that nothing happened."

"I know you're lying, you good-for-nothing whore!" he yelled. "If you don't admit it, I'll stab you and myself with this knife." He grabbed the knife and raised his hand over me.

"Please, Miguel." I begged for my life. "Please. Don't." My body trembled all over. I covered my face with my hands.

"Okay, fine. I will kill myself then," he said. He pointed the knife at his body.

I rose from my place on the floor and begged him to let go of it.

He thought for a brief second, then lowered the knife next to him. "Okay now, tell me. Did you have an affair with Peter?"

"No, there's no affair going on," I insisted.

"We will sit here until you admit there was an affair."

Hours ticked by as I sat there, my arms on my crossed legs, while Miguel dozed off in the chair. At 2 AM, he finally let me go to bed. I was shaken but relieved that nothing had happened.

***

The next morning, after speaking to my neighbor, Melissa, she tried to persuade me to leave with the children. She had heard Miguel yelling the previous night, and she feared for the safety of my children and me. She mentioned that she had been in an abusive relationship once and got the courage to leave her spouse with the help from a friend.

According to Melissa, domestic abuse wasn't a well-known crime publicly in 1987. If people heard a couple in a heated argument or fighting, they wouldn't step in to stop it because they believed it was a private family matter. However, at that time, there were domestic violence abuse shelters that women and children could go to if they needed to be in a safe environment.

"Jenny, do you want to go to a shelter?" Melissa asked.

"Maybe Miguel will stop threatening and interrogating me," I said. "I really shouldn't leave. I have no money and Hawai'i is two thousand miles away. How would we get home to O'ahu?"

"There's a way. Maybe your family can help you and the children get home?"

I tried to explain to Melissa that my family didn't have money to get plane tickets for Michael, Remie, and I to catch a flight to Hawai'i. I left her feeling sad and depressed.

When Miguel came home from work that evening, he threatened me again. He kept me up most of the night. I had a hard time trying to stay awake as he continued to interrogate me into the wee hours of the morning.

When my body slumped to the floor from being too tired, he'd pull me upright. Whenever he pulled at me, I would think about all the reasons why I couldn't get up and run away with our children.

I recalled the talk I had with Father Gary who had told me to stay with Miguel, and I wondered what my sisters who were nuns would say if we left Vallejo. I felt it would disgrace my family if their eldest child wasn't strong enough to face her husband's abuse. Hadn't Mom persevered in her marriage with Dad at all costs?

Could I run away if I had the chance? Miguel wasn't at home 24/7. But where would we go? I had no money to go anywhere and my hometown was two thousand miles away.

As the night went on and the interrogation continued, Miguel uncrossed his legs and got up. He grabbed my right arm and pulled me up off the ground.

It stunned me.

I tried to shake off my sleeplessness. As I steadily got to my feet, he jerked me so hard I was facing the bedroom with my back towards him.

Miguel shoved me toward our bedroom, closed the door, and pushed me hard onto the bed.

I pleaded with him to stop. "Please, no, Miguel… please, no!" I cried out over and over again, trying to push him away from me.

He was stronger than me, and I was weak after hours and hours of being interrogated.

"I don't want to do this now," I cried out. I had a sense of what he wanted to do to me.

But Miguel ignored my crying. He pulled my shorts and underwear down my legs.

"No!" I helplessly cried out. "No! Please, no!"

Miguel didn't stop. He held my arms down on the bed and assaulted me. I cried out and tried to resist, but he never stopped.

When it was over, I rolled on to my right side and cried. I really thought I could persevere everything that Miguel did; however, assaulting me was the last straw. I knew then and there that I wanted to leave with the children to somewhere "safe" from Miguel.

Chapter Three
Courage to Run

When I woke up a few hours later, Miguel had already left for work. I had had enough. Being raped by my husband was the final straw. If he had gone that far to hurt me because of something he suspected, what would he do next? I was scared for the well-being of my children and I.

Terrifying thoughts of him actually killing me crossed my mind. I didn't want Miguel to hurt our children, either. As a result, I sought out help from our neighbor.

In 1987, if a husband sexually assaulted his wife, it was recognized as being a legal act. Men would not get arrested for it. However, marital rape became illegal in 1993 throughout all 50 states. Those who were in higher risk of marital rape included women who were and are experiencing domestic abuse/violence, as well as those women who are making an attempt to leave their spouses.

I didn't know those details on that chilly October morning when I left my children watching television and went to Melissa's apartment. I knocked on her front door. I was desperate.

"I've had enough," I sniffled. "Can you please help us?"

"Oh, my god! What happened, Jenny?" Melissa asked. "Where's the children?"

All I could do was cry. I couldn't speak. I was too overwhelmed.

Melissa put her arms around me and let me cry.

Finally, after many minutes of tears slipping down my cheeks, I replied, "They're in my apartment watching TV."

Once I was settled on her sofa with a glass of water and tissues, she swiftly walked to the telephone and called the domestic violence abuse shelter.

After someone answered the phone on the other end, Melissa explained that a mother and two children in her neighborhood needed help and a safe place to go.

A long conversation ensued with the person telling Melissa the steps to take. She hung up the telephone and told me to go to my apartment and get birth certificates, Social Security cards, and any identification cards I had for myself and the children.

Calm now and more in control of my emotions, I returned to my apartment where Michael and Remie were still watching cartoons. I tried my best to search for the documents quietly, without raising concern from them. After finding what I needed, I shoved everything into a small black purse. At that moment, it dawned on me that Miguel could come home, and he would find us still in the apartment. I was extremely scared. I quickly looked around the apartment to make sure everything was where it should be, and I asked the children to come with me.

We met Melissa by the steps of her apartment, then quickly walked to her car. The drive to the designated place the worker from the shelter had mentioned was a quiet one. I hadn't told the children where we were going, only that Melissa needed to take us somewhere. All the while, troubling thoughts passed through my mind.

Would Miguel hunt us down and try to kill us as he had threatened he would?

I feared for our safety, but I also felt guilty about leaving our home and taking the children with me without telling him. I felt guilty. I repeatedly asked myself the same questions. *What would the Catholic Church do? Would they condemn me? What would my family in O'ahu think? Would they tell me to go back to Miguel?*

On top of all that, I had less than a dollar in my purse. I was worried what would happen to us. How would we eat? I took a deep breath to calm myself. The thought of Miguel raping me again, or the threats he made to me, were far more terrifying.

Sally from the shelter met Melissa, my children, and I about six miles away at a fast food restaurant. Sally ordered us drinks and spoke to Melissa, giving her instructions, and then asked me a lot of questions about the situation at home while Michael and Remie played in the jungle gym.

"You'll be okay," Melissa told me tearfully. "You are in safe hands."

Falling Perfectly Without Trying

"Thank you so much for helping us. I'm going to miss you!" I hugged her tightly and whispered in her ear, "Thank you for everything, my dear friend."

"You take care of yourself and those wonderful children of yours," she said.

After Melissa left, Sally took Michael, Remie, and I to her green station wagon. We all scrambled into her big car, and Sally drove us to a place where abused victims could stay temporarily.

Sally explained at great length that under no circumstances could anyone else know where the safe house was located. She also said I couldn't contact Miguel, because he might find us. If anyone knew where the safe house was, then it wouldn't be safe for anyone in the house to stay there.

We reached our destination and Sally drove the car into a garage next to a big brown house. A wooden fence and gate surrounded the house and it had a couple of big trees in the yard.

Inside, there were five bedrooms, two full bathrooms, a small kitchen, a dining room with an oak table and five chairs, and a living room with two worn-out brown leather sofas.

Two other families were living in the house. The two women had two young children each, and they welcomed us. Three female employees worked at the shelter. One of the women mentioned that there would be at least one employee who remained on site in the shelter at all times to make sure the victims were safe. It eased my mind.

Sally showed us to our room, which had a queen-sized bed with a flowery comforter and a white dresser. On the other side of the room stood a brown wooden closet with sliding doors. The room was decent and big enough for the three of us.

While Michael and Remie began making friends with the other children, another worker, Laurie, talked to me about what happened to bring my two children and I to the shelter. She explained the rules of the shelter and told us how things would work there.

As we chatted, I looked up on the wall and saw a big United Way sign. Laurie noticed and glanced at the sign. She mentioned that the organization helped sponsor the safe house, which surprised me. When I had worked for the bank in Hawai'i, I donated $20 every month to the Aloha United Way. It was a good feeling to know that United Way was helping us through a difficult time.

After an hour, one of the other staff members brought me a carton of eggs and some bread. She told me to cook something for my children and myself since it was close to dinner time.

I went into the kitchen and started cooking, but I felt really uneasy. I was lightheaded and almost burned the scrambled eggs. I took a deep breath, pulled myself together. I would get through this. Michael and Remie didn't question why we were there, because the relationship they had with their father was strained. Instead, they heartily ate the eggs and toast.

That night I slept well, not worrying if Miguel would wake me up in the middle of the night and threaten me.

The next day Laurie brought us to the state's

Department of Human Services, where I could apply for food stamps, financial assistance, and health care. Applying for state assistance was a complicated task for me, because there was so much paperwork involved. I wasn't used to asking for help or assistance in this way. My parents had never received benefits from the welfare system. My father always made enough to provide for us while he worked at a supermarket in O'ahu. Our family was big, and money was always tight. Yet, we managed to survive on Dad's paycheck.

After we returned to the shelter, the workers encouraged me to call my family in O'ahu.

"Mom, I left Miguel," I said quietly into the phone after Mom answered. "The children and I are at a domestic abuse shelter in California."

"Are you okay?" Mom asked. She sounded concerned.

"Yes, we're fine, but can we come home?" The thought of my family trying to scrape up enough money for us to fly from California to Hawai'i seemed an impossibility. With just Dad working, money was always tight. I didn't know how they'd ever find the money to bring Michael, Remie, and I back to Hawai'i.

"We'll try and get you all home soon, okay? I'll talk to Dad. I love you, Jenny. You take care of my grandchildren."

"I will," I said. "I love you, too, Mom."

Then my younger sister, Deanna, came on the phone. She was crying. She'd been so scared for her big sister thousands of miles away.

"Jenny, do you want to come home or do you want to

stay with Aunty Barbara and Uncle Sam in Monterey?" Deanna asked.

"I'm not sure. Maybe we can stay at the shelter for now," I said. "If we need to, we'll go to Monterey. I'm not well enough to travel."

My sister knew why I wasn't well. I had been suffering from two eating disorders, anorexia and bulimia, for a year. Living with Miguel had been difficult and stressful.

Before moving to California, I was impressed by my cousin, Delia Jean, who was a model. She was so beautiful, skinny, and famous, and I wanted to be like her. Instead of watching what I ate, counting calories and exercising, I became bulimic. I would eat whatever I wanted, but I was in the bathroom later, forcefully throwing up my food.

Later, with lots of people trying to discourage me from being bulimic, I instead swung to the other end of the spectrum and became anorexic, deliberately not eating at all. I went from weighing 150 pounds to 85 on the day we entered the shelter. I always felt lightheaded but didn't want to eat. I felt fat, which wasn't true. But whenever I looked at myself in the mirror, I'd see myself as being really fat. In reality, I was very thin.

After I called my family, I set a goal to get healthier and stronger because I wanted to go home. Trying to eat was difficult, especially since food wasn't particularly appetizing at the shelter.

We returned to the Department of Human Services, where the employees promised I would receive food stamps within the next few days.

"Then you can buy the kinds of food that you and your children would like to eat," Laurie said. She knew I was anorexic since I had admitted it to her that first day in the shelter.

Another complicated task was enrolling the children in an elementary school near the shelter. The school was two blocks away and I thought my children would be excited.

"Mom, do we have to go to this school?" Michael asked. "I miss our old school."

I explained, "It's just for a little while. It won't be forever."

"Are we going back to Hawai'i?" Michael said. "I want to go back already and see Grandma and Grandpa."

"Yes, we'll be going home soon," I said. "Before you know it, we'll be back in no time."

It saddened me that my children weren't happy, but I'd make it up to them as soon as I could.

"As soon as we have money, I'll buy you some toys," I said. "Okay, Michael?"

While Michael and I were talking, Remie overheard us.

"Alright, Mom," Remie said, "can I have another popple?"

"Yes, I'll get you another one," I answered. "But, please go to school."

We reached the school gates and walked through it. I had to show them where their classes were, so I brought each of them to see their teacher and kissed their cheeks as I said good-bye.

"I love you," I said. "Be good now. I'll be back after school."

Then I left and walked back to the shelter. I talked to Laurie as well as the main person who oversaw the shelter, Maryann.

"I hope you will like it here," Maryann said. "It's very quiet, especially when the children are in school. Maybe you can plan for the future?"

"Yes, I like it here very much. Everyone is super nice and considerate. I can use this free time to figure out what I'm going to do next. I know we're going back to Hawai'i, but I don't know when."

Knowing that my children and I were going back to live with my parents made me happy. As we settled in our new environment, I became less frightened and more at ease with our living arrangements. I still had horrible dreams at night and was worried that Miguel would find us, but he hadn't yet. The shelter workers, particularly Laurie, took time to talk to me, which helped a lot.

Our first food stamps came within two days, and Sally brought the children and I to the grocery store. I was surprised to find out that I could buy all kinds of food and snacks for the three of us.

The next day, Laurie set up an appointment with a therapist for me, knowing I suffered from eating disorders and post-traumatic stress. She and I had talked about what happened the day I slumped to the floor and became cold and incoherent.

"You were experiencing a nervous breakdown, also known as a chemical imbalance," she said. "Women who go through such terrifying experiences may also have a nervous breakdown, but it's different for each individual."

While we talked about what Miguel did to me, I brought up how I felt about being in a safe house.

"Miguel threatened me daily for two months, but he didn't physically hurt us," I told her. "He yelled, called me all kinds of names, ridiculed me, put me down, threw things at me, and expressed excessive jealousy towards me. However, my children and I don't have any scars or knife wounds or bullet holes in our bodies. Why, after all the threats and interrogation, did we never get hurt physically?"

"Because you never fought back," Laurie explained. "Women get hurt because they fight back against their abuser, and you didn't."

I learned that emotional abuse is considered the worst kind of abuse. When a person is emotionally abused, the scars are long lasting and very hard to erase, according to "Intimate" Violence Against Women.

Laurie mentioned that she had a boyfriend who was originally from Hawai'i. She knew how everyone was part of one big 'Ohana'—family in Hawai'i. Everyone treated one another the way they wanted to be treated. She was worried for us, though. Hawai'i was so far away.

***

Two weeks later, worried about Peter's (the mailman) safety, I wrote a letter to him telling him I was sorry that Miguel accused us of having an affair. (I admit now that I did have a crush on the man, but nothing happened between us. We were friends only.) I mailed the letter with no return address at a nearby post office.

A week later, the shelter employees ordered me to get Michael and Remie out of school immediately because Miguel had visited the school office and asked for his children. The employees weren't sure how he had found the neighborhood as well as the school the children attended.

They decided it would be best if they transferred Michael, Remie, and I to another shelter in a different district. When we returned from school, our few belongings had been packed and Sally told us to get in the car.

I was so terrified. The children were crying because they didn't want to leave another school and their new friends. They had been adjusting to their living arrangements, and the thought of leaving had scared them.

Sally drove us 10 miles away to a different shelter. Our new shelter was nothing like the old one. The yard was filled with tall weeds, and the inside of the house was in disarray. It didn't have as many chairs, tables, or beds. We were told there weren't enough workers to manage that particular safe house 24/7, so there would be times we would be alone in the house. The refrigerator wasn't well-stocked with food; in fact, there was a swollen sausage sitting in a big jar of water on the top rack of the ice box. Since I didn't bring any food with us to the shelter, one of the workers gave me

Falling Perfectly Without Trying

a can of tuna to feed ourselves.

Laurie called a few hours later to check in on us.

"I'm so sorry that they sent you and your children to that run-down safe house, Jenny," she said. "If I had been on duty, I would have made other arrangements. Why don't you call your aunty and uncle in Monterey so that they can help you and the children until you can go back to Hawai'i?"

"I'll call them right away. It sounds better than staying at this place," I told Laurie.

As scared as I was, I called Aunty Barbara and told her that Michael, Remie, and I were living in a safe house, but it was a rundown place. I asked if we could stay with her in Monterey for a while until my mom and siblings could raise the money to get us home.

After a minute or two of talking with her, she volunteered to pay our bus fare to Monterey the next evening. It was a heartwarming call. I appreciated that my aunt was willing to have us live with them for a while.

The next afternoon, a social worker at the shelter loaded two boxes with our belongings into a station wagon and drove us to a nearby bus transit center. She helped us unload our boxes and left, leaving us to wait for the bus to Monterey.

I was weak and had a difficult time moving the boxes closer to the bus that we had to board. My children were too young to assist me, but I didn't want to leave our belongings. I looked around and spotted a young boy just hanging out.

"Ma'am, do you need help?" he asked. "I would

help you if you gave me a few dollars."

"That's great," I replied without hesitation. "I sure could use some help."

The boy picked up the boxes and put them where the luggage was stored under the bus. However, in the chaos of leaving, I forgot to give him his money. I felt bad as we sat in the bus while the boy looked at us from outside.

We reached Monterey in two hours and thirty minutes. Aunty Barbara and Uncle Sam welcomed us with open arms.

"You all made it," she said, hugging each of us tightly. "I'm so glad you are all safe."

"Thank you for taking us in, Aunty Barbara," I said. "I will never forget your kindness and generosity."

Aunty Barbara and Uncle Sam helped carry the two large boxes to their car. Then, Uncle Sam drove us to their house.

While riding in the back seat of their car, I felt relieved that Michael, Remie, and I were no longer homeless. Loving relatives had willingly invited us into their home and lives. I was still afraid that Miguel would find us, but for the moment we were "safe."

As Uncle Sam stopped the car in the driveway at their house, we could hear dogs barking. Michael and Remie immediately became alarmed.

"Don't worry," Aunty Barbara said. "They don't bite. They bark and get excited when we have guests come to the house."

Indeed, when we got into the house, the dogs kept wanting to jump on us.

Falling Perfectly Without Trying

Their house had three bedrooms, a living room, dining room, kitchen, two bathrooms, and a room where the washer and dryer were kept. It was a cozy house with beautiful furniture. We felt comfortable in Aunty Barbara's house.

The next day, I enrolled Michael and Remie in an elementary school nearby. While the children were in school, I tried to get food stamps again from the welfare office in Monterey's City and County offices. The office workers were very nice and understanding, and they helped me with the application for food stamps, financial and medical benefits for the three of us.

As our lives got to some normalcy, I was still worried Miguel would find us. After a week had passed, Miguel found out where we were and called the house.

"You better come home, Jenny," Miguel said. "No one will want to take care of you and the children after a while. If you don't come home, I'll drive to Monterey and kill you and the children."

Miguel kept calling and threatening me every day. I was extremely frightened, because I believed our lives were in danger.

Aunty Barbara feared for our safety as well as their own. When the threats didn't diminish and as everyone's lives were at stake, I knew it was time to make an exit. I quietly made arrangements with my family to return to Hawai'i.

Somehow, my parents and siblings had gotten the money together to bring us home. I was so happy that I jumped up and down and clapped my hands a few times when Mom told me the news.

Jenny Duhaylonsod Delos Santos

We were flying back the day after Thanksgiving. I was ready and prepared to face everyone back home. It was a relief, but I also felt guilty. Leaving my husband and our life in California made me feel like I had failed. Despite everything that happened in Vallejo, in the eyes of the church, it was wrong for me to leave Miguel and end our marriage.

But no matter how I felt, my family said they wanted me home, particularly since I was still dealing with eating disorders and in no condition to argue with Miguel. The children's safety was a top priority. It was better to go back to O'ahu to be in the safety net of my parents' home.

I had only been with Uncle Sam and Aunty Barbara for thirty days. Emotionally, I was sad yet happy when Aunty Barbara and Uncle Sam brought Michael, Remie, and I to the San Diego International Airport. I hugged them good-bye as tears rolled down my cheeks.

My five-year-old daughter carried her purple stuffed animal in her left hand and six-year-old Michael held unto his blue toy truck in his right hand as the three of us boarded the plane.

Michael climbed unto the seat next to the window, and I helped Remie scramble unto the seat on my left side. The stewardesses made sure all the other passengers were safely in their seats while the pilots gave the directions that they were ready to take off.

I looked lovingly at Michael, who had blue jeans and a black t-shirt on. His hair was cut short, and he wore white sneakers. As for Remie, she wore a short sleeve yellow dress that had ruffles on the bottom seam with

Falling Perfectly Without Trying

white sandals on her feet. Her black hair was a little past her shoulders and she was petite for her age. Both children were happy to be going back to Hawai'i.

During most of the five-hour flight to O'ahu, Michael and Remie slept in their seats as I looked upon them. I was at peace with myself knowing that we'd soon be thousands of miles away from Miguel.

All of those years of being in a domestic violence relationship with Miguel had taken a toll on me. Despite what I felt, Michael, Remie, and I couldn't wait to reach our destination.

Chapter Four
Home Sweet Home

Michael, Remie, and I were joyously reunited with my family at Honolulu International Airport, now named the Daniel K. Inouye International Airport.

"It's such a relief to be home," I said to my mom, Donna, as we hugged each other tight. "I will never go back to Miguel ever again."

"We are here to take care of you now, but it's up to you what you want to do," she replied. "I'm just glad you are all safe and in Hawai'i."

As my parents drove us to their house in 'Ewa Beach, I felt so relieved. I was happy to be home and surrounded by people who loved me and my children unconditionally. We would be safe as long as we were in Hawai'i.

We settled in at my parents' house in 'Ewa Beach over the next few weeks, and I arranged for Michael and Remie to attend Kaimiloa Elementary School. They were delighted to go to the same school as their cousin, Cheryl, who was two years younger than Michael. They didn't feel lost or left out when they went to their classes.

Falling Perfectly Without Trying

As for Miguel, he kept calling me to say that he was coming back to Hawai'i to kill us. He continued to threaten me about shooting Michael, Remie, and my immediate family. I was scared for my life and of those around me. His words affected me so much that I started getting psychologically sick.

We didn't have caller ID, so I never knew who was calling when I picked up the phone. Whenever he managed to get me, I was terrified during the entire conversation, even though he was over two thousand miles away. My voice quivered and my heart raced. I'd sweat all over; my body would shake. I had a hard time taking normal breaths. It wasn't long before I felt chest pains, became nauseated, and had a fear of going crazy. I felt a sense of impending doom. I experienced small nervous breakdowns every time he called.

Fortunately, my sister, Bertha, had experience with dealing with mental illness. She'd spent some time in a convent and knew some nuns who suffered from anxiety disorders. She knew how to help me get through those phone calls. If it wasn't for her, my parents probably would've sent me to the hospital because they weren't sure what to do.

After a few weeks, I had an appointment to get professional help from a psychiatrist and therapist, who diagnosed me with acute anxiety disorder and post-traumatic stress. Miguel's threats and interrogations disabled me to the point of needing continuous psychological treatments over many years.

I applied for welfare benefits again. It wasn't easy to get help in Hawai'i, since I'd received food stamps in California. It was an uphill battle trying to convince the State Department of Human Services that I wasn't returning to California and intended to stay in Hawai'i was difficult to do.

The state welfare employees finally believed me when they got the paperwork through the mail from California's Department of Human Services. We received food stamps, free medical, and financial aid. I knew Mom and Dad would help me as much as they could, but I needed to start being independent. I had the opportunity to attend some classes at a YWCA in downtown Honolulu two weeks later.

The classes were essentially a support group to help welfare clients decide what direction to pursue. Many of the women came from traumatic experiences and needed guidance and support. I received a lot of support from the program's instructors and students. A month had passed since we had returned from California, and I was still shaken up. Psychologically, I was wiped out. The support group was like an *ohana*—family to me during those two months.

Several months after I finished my classes, I visited the Legal Aid Society of Hawai'i to seek a divorce from Miguel. It was a long process applying for help and having the paralegal draft a divorce decree. Trying to put my married life behind me made me emotional. As I spoke to my lawyer and paralegal about what had happened in California, I would end up crying describing my circumstances.

The day came for my lawyer and I to appear before the judge. I was a nervous wreck.

Falling Perfectly Without Trying

As we both headed to the judge's chambers, Miguel came up next to me and handed a note over to me. It said, *You are going to hell!*

The gesture made me cry uncontrollably, to the point that my lawyer told me to stay outside in the hallway. She'd talk to the judge, so I wouldn't have to go into court.

It seemed like many hours passed by while I waited, even though the proceedings only took a half hour. My lawyer emerged and told me that the divorce proceedings would continue after I attended counseling sessions in Waikiki for domestic abuse survivors.

I attended the Maluhia 'O Wahine Curriculum at the Waikiki Community Center and met many other women who had been abused by their significant others. Some of them still lived with their abusers, while others had just left their homes. The women felt comfortable in that environment, and soon opened up to one another about their experiences.

In just a few days, I learned many things about being in an abusive and violent relationship, as well as what an abuser is capable of doing to the victim.

In a booklet I received during one session, I noticed a chart that looked like a wheel. Each *spoke* represented a tactic that the abuser used to control or gain power. The rim that surrounded the spokes represented *physical abuse*, and it held the system together and gave it strength. When control or power tactics failed, the abuser would try threatening or using physical abuse to gain control of the relationship.

Those tactics were explained something like this in the wheel:

> **Being isolated** - The abuser controls what the victim does, whom she can see as well as talk to and where she can go.

> **Using their children** - The abuser makes the victim feel guilty about their children as well as tells the children to give messages to their parent, who isn't cooperative.

> **Economic abuse** - The abuser forces the victim to ask for money, takes money away from her and/or tries to keep their spouse from obtaining or holding a job.

> **Intimidation** - The abuser makes the victim become fearful by showing her awful faces when looking at her, talking to her loudly, smashing things, and destroying her property to intimidate her.

> **Sexual abuse** - The abuser makes the victim do sexual acts against her will and treats her like a sex object.

> **Emotional abuse** - The abuser calls the victim all kinds of names, plays mind games with her, and/or makes her feel bad about herself.

> **Using male privileges** - The abuser treats the victim like a servant and acts like the "master of the castle."

> **Threats** - The abuser will threaten to take the children away from the victim, commit suicide, or harm her. If all else fails, the abuser may carry out the threats to hurt and control her.

As I listened to the instructors as they mentioned

these different tactics, I realized how much Miguel used the Power and Control wheel over me to keep command of our relationship. How I had ever had the courage to leave Miguel is a miracle. Even with my friends and family's support, it was a decision I had to make by myself.

Attending the family violence program made me mentally stronger and capable of going through with the divorce. I was still scared of Miguel and experienced PTSD, but I could put a wall up in front of me whenever he came too close to me or threatened me.

On April 23, 1990, two years after leaving him, Miguel and I were granted a divorce. I had sole custody of Michael and Remie. I was happy, and my family and friends were relieved. Everyone who knew me knew he had abused me. We were better off without him, many of family members said.

As for child support, I didn't want anything from him except a divorce and life without him. His threats were enough for me to ask for nothing and run away, hoping never to talk to him ever again. My lawyer tried to convince me that it was mandatory under Hawai'i law to ask for at least $10 per child. We ended up settling for the minimum amount.

Even though I could finally put my marriage behind me, I had another hurdle to cross. I had to request an annulment from the Catholic Church.

Chapter Five
Moving On

A few months went by, and with the help of the Department of Human Services, I attended the Employment Training Office, a clerical school that was run by the State of Hawai'i. The school was located in Honolulu, a few blocks from the Ala Moana Shopping Mall, walking distance for me to get to.

Many of the ETO students were welfare recipients like myself, who wanted clerical training. The instructors taught the basics to prepare us for office work. While I had many years of experience already, not working for almost a decade had made me unsure of my skills and capabilities. ETO helped me to practice daily on a typewriter, calculator, and telephone, which made me feel much more comfortable about my skills and more at ease being among other people.

The instructors were very supportive, constantly explaining things in easy steps to me and making me feel positive about myself.

A counselor was assigned to have a session with me a few times a week. The counselor wasn't a therapist or a psychologist, but more like a friend who would

Falling Perfectly Without Trying

listen to all my problems, as well as what happened in my daily life and give me advice on how to handle those situations. The support they gave me helped me balance my life and be able to succeed beyond ETO.

I got to intern at a nonprofit organization in Kalihi. I felt uneasy being away from the positive atmosphere the school fostered. But as the hours and days went by, I settled in and found I could work in an office again. My dream of being self-sufficient and supporting my children with the income I made was more than enough to make me feel I could succeed.

There was a government agency who coordinated with ETO to help underprivileged students, giving $50 every two weeks for professional clothing. Even I, who couldn't afford to buy new clothes on the welfare money I received every month, could buy skirts, blouses, and jackets for my job. It was such a blessing.

Within six months as an ETO student, I landed a transcriber position at a mortgage company in downtown Honolulu. I was so proud to finally be able to live out my dream of self-sufficiency. I still lived with my parents, but I could afford to buy clothes, toys, and miscellaneous items for my children and myself, which I had been barely able to afford on welfare benefits.

Working at the mortgage company helped me to be more positive about myself and more confident in my job as a word transcriber. Not only could I type super-fast and with ease, but I was highly proficient.

The company I worked for was huge, and I made many friends in the department I worked in as well as on other floors of the company. During the holidays, we had big department and company parties, including a get together at a hotel in Waikiki. I had so much fun!

My life was almost complete.

I had met an Asian male friend, Albert. He gave me roses and bought me beautiful gifts, including boxes of Sees candies, a black silk dress, and other clothing from a shop located in downtown Honolulu. Albert also bought me perfume and cosmetics, as well as getting together for lunch whenever I could get away from the office.

I was so touched by his sincere generosity and so infatuated with him. Being with Albert was so different than ever being with Miguel. Albert always made me happy when I was with him.

Albert was the first boyfriend I had after my divorce. As a result, I felt very special whenever I got a gift from him. I had never had so much positive attention from one individual, so when my co-workers told me to end the relationship with him, I felt guilty for doing so. They said he wasn't an "angel." Besides me, Albert had two other girlfriends that he dated. One of the women was a teacher at a local elementary school and the other woman was a lawyer at a prestigious law firm. Both ladies were single with no children.

Here I was with two children, recently divorced, and living with my parents in 'Ewa Beach. I realized that I wasn't ready for a commitment, and Albert was unwilling to have only one girlfriend.

So, after days and days of talking it over with him, I ended our relationship. I was very emotional, but I thought it was the best thing to do under the circumstances. However, we continued to remain friends.

Two years passed.

I continued my work for the mortgage company. My children were doing well, happy, and enjoying school. However, I hadn't addressed my psychological problems or my ongoing illnesses—post-traumatic stress and anorexia.

One day, I got into a heated argument with a co-worker when the manager of the department was not in the office. All of the sudden, my heart raced, I was sweating, and my body was shaking. I had a hard time breathing, I was nauseated, and I had chest pains. I started to hyperventilate. I didn't know what was happening. I went under an empty desk and shook. Some of my co-workers were concerned and tried to coax me into coming out from under the desk, but I couldn't stop shaking or crying. I couldn't calm my emotions down.

Eventually, the department's assistant manager called for an ambulance to take me to the hospital. By the time the emergency technicians came into the office, I had already passed out due to hyperventilation, and lay on the carpet under the desk.

When I woke up, I was laying on a hospital bed in the emergency room. I couldn't comprehend what had happened.

Bertha was sitting next to me and explained what had happened. I got upset again, worried about what would happen with my job, and she comforted me.

The ER doctor diagnosed me with acute anxiety disorder, treatable with psychiatric help, medicine, and therapy. He wanted to keep me in the hospital for a few days for evaluation and until I could do things on my own.

Because of the severity of my situation, I couldn't do any normal daily activities on my own, including be able to walk to the bathroom or even brush my hair. I couldn't think straight and constantly had the feeling of impending doom. Many times, the fear of dying went through my thoughts until the nurses on the psychiatric floor convinced me that I was healthy and fine.

Three days later, I was able to go home, but it was clear it would take months before I would overcome the disorder.

I began to experience symptoms similar to vertigo; I felt uneasy when I walked, as if the floor was moving under me. I couldn't understand why everything I did felt like I was doing it backwards.

I voluntarily quit my job after a few weeks, realizing I was mentally unable to return. I applied for state help again and found a good psychiatrist and a therapist to help me overcome my acute anxiety disorder and to deal with the post-traumatic stress.

It was around this time that I asked Miguel to come back to O'ahu. He had stopped threatening me while I worked at the mortgage company and we were on better terms with each other. Even though I wasn't psychologically healed yet, I wanted him to be around his children, who kept asking for him.

Remie had started having terrible tantrums. She

Falling Perfectly Without Trying

attacked Michael and I on an almost daily basis. One time, she flipped me right over her when I was trying to get her into the car to see a psychiatrist. Another time, Mom, Michael, and I all had to hold down Remie, because she was having an extremely bad tantrum. But, we couldn't hold her down. As a result, a neighbor had to help us. It was a scary ordeal.

Finally, her psychiatrist suggested to me that the best place for Remie was at Leahi Hospital, which was a psychiatric hospital for children. She would be hospitalized for three months.

While Remie was in Leahi, her psychiatrist, my family, and many of my friends encouraged me to ask for an application for an annulment through the Catholic Church. Everyone close to me knew what Miguel had done to me, and they convinced me that an annulment would be granted if I wrote down everything that had happened in California.

This is a process I had started several times, but trying to describe everything on paper, particularly what happened while living with him in California, was like reliving that disturbing part of my life all over again. I couldn't go to that place in my mind where those memories were stored. I had post-traumatic stress and cried a lot during the process. But with everyone's support, I finally completed the application. It was a relief, particularly because I had mixed emotions about leaving him, but asking for a divorce and now filing for annulment, I realized, would be a good thing.

Several months later, I received the letter from the church granting the annulment. It was a happy day as tears rolled down my face as I read it. Words couldn't describe the mixed emotions I felt as I received that news.

***

When Miguel returned to Hawai'i, he lived with his parents in Mililani. He'd come over to see his children every so often. He also talked to me when he visited, but I was still afraid of him. He tried to convince me to come back to him for the children's sake.

I couldn't. I wouldn't go back to that dark place again, even if he promised to treat me better.

However, these moments with him led to my renewed psychological illness and hospitalization for the month of April. I was first admitted to the Queen's Medical Center Emergency Room. I was very sick and not mentally all there.

A security guard told me that I was acting like a child. "Every time the doctor talk to you, you say the word ice cream!"

Every time someone spoke of Miguel, I would crouch into a little ball and go in the corner of the room. It was hard to keep me on the bed. Eventually, they were able to calm me down. Bertha came in the room, and her presence helped. Just by her talking to me, I would then calm down and lay on the bed.

In an old journal I kept, I had written down these words.

Becoming a little girl was like a way out from all my problems, because little girls don't worry about anything. When I act like a little girl, it's like I'm watching the scene play out from above (near the ceiling) and I can see everything happening. It feels like my mind is somehow detached from my body. Like my life is some kind of play.

While I was in the emergency room, the attending ER doctor advised me to go to Kekela, a psychiatric unit as well as a safe place for people experiencing mental illness symptoms.

At first, I was scared to be in Kekela because of the negativity people expressed when talking about psych wards. I had heard so many bad stories.

However, while I was there, I met some incredible patients who truly had problems. Others had trouble coping psychologically and just needed somewhere safe to live for a while. I befriended many patients during that month and got used to being in the psychiatric ward. I got along well with the staff, and they were very nice to me. I had worried for no reason.

According to my psychiatrist, I had psychoneurosis with anxiety and conversion disorder features. It was also confirmed that I had dissociation features and post-traumatic stress, which of course I knew. I learned that because I felt I couldn't control my life, my bulimia/anorexia disorders had become something I could control. It took years of psychiatric therapy for me to feel healthy in mind and body and not focus on how I looked. A lot of support from my family and friends helped me to conquer my eating disorders.

Much later, I learned the specifics of all of those illnesses. Psychoneurosis with anxiety is characterized by disturbed social relationships, as well as inner struggles. The attacks are precipitated by emotional stresses, conflicts, frustrations, and stresses. The attacks are not produced by physical disorders. Some of the symptoms include the inability to concentrate or make decisions, have morbid doubts, shortness of breath, fatigue, headaches and multiple pains and aches. I had most of those symptoms.

Dissociation helps people cope with a traumatic event by providing a mechanism for them to defend against overwhelming emotions. In most cases, dissociation features are triggered by trauma. My curling into a ball was one of my coping mechanisms.

Post-traumatic stress is when the victim relives the traumatic events in their lives through memory "triggers" or flashbacks. Those who are afflicted with the disease can be treated through psychiatry and/or psychotherapy, which may take years and years to recover from. This is what I was learning to do every day.

While I was in Kekela, the nurses encouraged me to keep a daily journal of things that happened while I was in the hospital. One nurse gave me a new composition notebook so I could write notes and look at it later.

The best person who helped me was the psychiatrist, I wrote in my journal. *Just by...being here a couple of days...the doctor was able to explain why I was sick all the time.*

I lived with fear and pain daily. I would often feel and act like a four-year-old girl. Life was too hard to face for me, according to the psychiatrist.

I would have a flashback of what happened in California, then old, sad memories would run through my mind. Because it was so traumatic, I would feel symptoms of nausea and dizziness, I couldn't walk or talk, and would sometimes hyperventilate. By the end of the episode, I talked and acted like a little girl, because when I was little, I didn't have to face life like a grownup.

The psychiatrists and nurses at Kekela helped me to understand what was going on with my mind and body and why it was happening. One psychiatric assistant told me, "When you are experiencing similar situations or hear similar words that trigger past experiences and painful thoughts, you must use learned coping skills when you recognize warning signs or symptoms. Calming yourself down will help minimize anxiety attacks or possible overwhelming feelings. Convince yourself that the past is the past and will always be the past."

I enrolled in therapeutic classes as well as classes that taught patients how to survive with a mental illness in the outside world. There were also art classes where I drew many pictures that expressed how I felt on the inside.

In my journal, I wrote, *I felt very happy, surprised and shocked to realize that people would actually accept me for what I really am. So much was said positively at art therapy. It made me realize that I didn't look ugly with glasses on and they like me as I am.*

With help from the Kekela staff, I got stronger physically and psychologically. Eventually, I was able to face Miguel and tell him that I didn't want to go back to living with him ever again.

I had asked my family and church friends to pray that I may overcome my fears he invoked and to be able to be strong enough to talk to him. When that day came—April 26—I felt like a lot of people were praying for me, because I felt this certain energy force within me.

At 2 PM, Miguel came into the visiting room at the hospital, and I was able to say whatever I had to say to him that day without my wall breaking down as what usually happened.

I said, "Miguel, you are a good person and a good father; however, I cannot go back to you. I do forgive you, but all the pain I felt during the years we were married has scarred my heart forever. If I go back to you without any love in my heart, I would probably make you unhappier because I wouldn't give or show you any love. You would feel your heart dying, because I would deny you the love that you want and need. I have thought about going back to you for the kids' sake, but I know I would repeat another mistake. If I didn't have the kids, I would never dream of living with you again."

Being with him for a half hour and having to say so many things was scary. I wanted to faint. But, I handled the situation without falling to pieces. He didn't have much to say in response. After he left, Mom and my sisters came to visit.

For a while, I really considered this place (Kekela) my home, because of all the support, friendship, and love that I received here," I wrote in my journal. *"However, last night I realized that I can bring all that love, support, and friendship back to my real home—in 'Ewa Beach.*

Before I departed Kekela, a few people wrote in my journal, but there was one note that stood out.

Always remember how special you are. How full of love and sensitive you are, also. Follow the white dove to freedom, and may you be protected by the light, a psychiatric aide wrote. *I respect how hard you work and know you will be successful with patience and time.*

Soon, the medical staff felt I was ready to face life beyond Kekela. I had successfully accomplished what I had intended to do. I wasn't cured from all my ailments, but I was stronger and more in control of my illnesses than before.

Another chapter of my life was finally over.

***

Two months later, my life changed for the better. I began getting involved with the Catholic Church, Our Lady of Perpetual Help Church, again. I became a Sunday school teacher, as well as helped with the teens who were active in the Filipino Catholic Club. We had meetings and organized a spiritual weekend, which was held at St. Stephen's Seminary.

Besides volunteering at church, I had met someone very special. His name was Rusty and he was a year younger than I was, single and never married, with no children. He lived with his family (his mom, sister, nieces and nephews) in 'Ewa Beach and was very artistic. He could draw well and make Hawaiian jewelry out of Koa wood, buffalo bone, fish hooks, and other natural items.

At first, Rusty and I were close friends that liked to talk to each other a lot, but as the days and months went by, he started treating me more than just a friend.

"Jenny, why don't we go to Roy's Restaurant in Kapolei," Rusty asked one afternoon. "We can go there Friday night. They have really good tender-raised beef short ribs."

"That sounds great," I said. "But, what will I wear? All my dresses are out of date and too old to wear."

Rusty had an answer for that, too. He immediately responded, "I can bring you to that place at Pearl Ridge tomorrow? If you find a real nice dress at the store, I'll pay for it."

I was amazed that Rusty was willing to buy me a dress and pay for dinner.

"Alright," I agreed happily. "Let's go tomorrow night to get a dress."

The next night, Rusty picked me up in his vehicle, and we went to the Pearl Ridge Shopping Mall. I found a beautiful red silk evening dress that Rusty thought looked nice on me. So, he bought it.

On Friday, he finished work early, and he came to pick me up at my parents' house where I was patiently waiting for him.

He stepped up to the front door with three roses in his hand, which was decorated with red silky ribbons and baby's breath flowers.

"Wow…that's for me?" I asked. "It's so pretty. Thank you."

I handed the flowers to Mom, who was standing nearby, and asked if she could put the flowers in a vase on the table.

Then we drove to Roy's Restaurant. We had a really nice time and the food was delicious.

A couple of days later, Mom told me to ask the Department of Human Services to send me to school. She had heard on the news that many welfare clients were seeking higher education, and she thought I would benefit from it if I went back to school.

After giving it much thought, I asked someone at the Department of Human Services about going to college. They were prepared to help me with paperwork and supported the idea of sending me to a community college.

"After you go to school, you'll be able to become self-sufficient and support your children and yourself on your income," said my social worker. "It's not easy though, but you'll make it."

I was determined to succeed in college, particularly because I had never received an education beyond high school. With persistence, and dreams of obtaining a degree and becoming self-sufficient, I applied to Leeward Community College.

A few weeks later, I received an acceptance letter. I could start school during the upcoming semester. However, I had to come to campus to take a couple of tests to determine what classes I could attend.

I had to take a math and English test, which would

determine my grade level of learning. When I found out that my tests were in the fourth-grade level, I was really depressed, however I was eligible to attend LCC's PASS Program.

In those first days of classes, it was difficult to attend classes and do all the homework that was required. I hadn't studied in such a long time. After a week of school, I got used to getting up early, attending classes, and going home to study.

I realized the instructors and professors in the PASS Program worked as a team to support the students, so the students could overcome many challenges. The program laid the foundation the students needed to be successful while pursuing their degrees.

There were many students in the PASS program who were parents receiving welfare benefits or were enrolled in another state program called JOBS (Job Opportunities and Basic Skills Training). One of the benefits of the JOBS program included being able to afford to pay for babysitters to watch their children while they were at school or work. Having that benefit gave student-parents less to worry about so they could concentrate on their studies.

JOBS, which was under the umbrella of the Department of Human Services, was designed to help recipients become self-sufficient and successful. The staff would assist their clients with educational help and counseling and prepare them for finding jobs. The social worker would start a career plan with their clients, who followed through with the plan. If problems arose, the social worker would be there to sort it out and help.

Falling Perfectly Without Trying

However, like many state projects, the federal government began cutting aid that supported organizations like the JOBS program. So social workers had to demand that students work part-time and go to school full-time. I was one of those students. I found a part-time job at LCC's library, which was great because it was located on campus.

It was difficult on me—to work, attend school, and take care of my kids, because by then, we had moved out of my parents' house and to the "Twin Towers," a pair of condominium towers about a mile away from LCC.

But I was determined to become self-sufficient and not depend on the state or my parents or anyone else to help me. I overcame all the obstacles of being a single parent raising two children, going to school full-time, and working part-time.

While I was at LCC, I was so busy that I barely had time to take care of my two children. Many times, I had to leave Michael and Remie with a neighbor in the afternoon so that I could work or attend a class. Michael didn't mind, but Remie didn't take it well. She was still seeing a therapist every two weeks and becoming more and more upset with me for not having time for them.

Despite those challenges, I enjoyed going to LCC and working at the library. I also wrote for the school paper, *Ka Mana'o*. Math was the hardest of my classes, but I excelled in English. During my first semester in the PASS program, I focused on my writing skills and explored jobs that would require professional writing. All I really knew was clerical jobs. As a result, my goal was to be an administrative assistant in a good environment and make at least $1,800.00 a month. I began striving towards two degrees: Administrative Assistant and Information Processing Specialist.

Because I was focused on my goals and dreams, it helped to be a good student. I appreciated the encouragement and support I received from the PASS Program instructors. I thought my English instructor was the best teacher I'd ever had. He wrote thoughtful notes on all of my assignments, which helped me with my writing.

There was one English assignment called "My Journal" that I kept, and it was dated April 20. At the end of the journal, my teacher wrote, *I gave you 111% for this assignment. You're a fine student, a fine writer, and a fine young woman. I'm certain you'll do well and remain well in your future.*

I kept that assignment hidden away in my pile of important papers and would look at it on occasion. I'd read it once in a while when things were tough, during times I needed the encouragement. After I read his words, I'd find an inner strength in me to keep on going with life, no matter the seriousness my obstacles and challenges were.

In my journal, I asked myself, *Will I be able to handle all the courses I signed up for next semester? Will my classes be too hard? Will the teachers be strict? Will my new instructors be as kind and hospitable as my PASS instructors were? Am I going to make it? Will I get sick again? Will I have the support that I need on the outside, as I have received in the PASS program?*

Falling Perfectly Without Trying

Will I ever be okay? Will I ever be normal? Am I going to recover from anorexia and bulimia someday? Is my anxiety disorder ever going to disappear and never come back to haunt me again? Will I find and meet nice students in my other classes? Will I ever have self-confidence again? Will I ever work again?"

The list went on. I had so much unanswered questions running through my mind that I didn't know how I'd ever make it through my second semester.

I signed up for regular college courses in the second semester, which included an English 100 class as well as journalism, political science, and philosophy classes. I was surprised that I had such an easy time writing for my classes, and my professors started asking me questions I hadn't expected to get.

"Who wrote your essay homework for you, Jenny?" my English instructor asked one day. "I don't believe you wrote it."

"I promise you that I did," I said. "I like to write. It's easy for me."

I got similar comments from other teachers. During my second semester at LCC, a political science professor returned an essay with no grade and no red marks on it, which confused me.

"I can't give you a grade for this essay," he said. "There's nothing wrong with it. I remember you said you don't have good grades when you try to write newspaper articles. Why don't you write something like a newspaper article for me?"

I continued to be praised by my professors and received A's in most of my classes. As a result, I began exploring different kinds of jobs that required writing and what my options were. I, in turn, asked my instructors questions about different job possibilities I could apply for, which made me very inquisitive.

While trying to excel in my classes and become the best student I could be, Remie became more and more distant from me. Being left alone with her brother, or sometimes by herself for a long time was too much for her. At times, she had to cook for the two of them. I tried to send her to the neighbor's while I wasn't home, but she didn't want to stay at the neighbor's place anymore.

I didn't realize just how troubled she was.

***

I reached my third semester at LCC, and with the help of the professors at Leeward Community College, I managed to focus on another dream: becoming a newspaper reporter. I knew it would take a lot of studying, dedication, and persistence from me, and support from numerous people in order for this to happen. Trying to obtain a bachelor's degree in journalism while being a single mother, living on my own with two children, working two part-time jobs, and writing articles for the school newspaper was not an overnight accomplishment. It would take a long time, and I would face many challenges.

Leeward Community College is one out of ten campuses in the University of Hawaii system. Founded in 1907, the University of Hawaii at Manoa is the main campus within the university's system. Faculty and students come from all over the world to take advantage of the research opportunities, athletics program, diverse community and beautiful campuses that the university provides.

When it came time to transfer from Leeward Community College to the University of Hawai'i at Manoa campus, I had some big decisions to make, including moving closer to the campus. Moving to Honolulu would make it difficult for my family in 'Ewa Beach to help with my children. As a result, I had to make up my mind on whether to send Michael to live with his dad in Mililani.

I couldn't live on my own with two children while attending UH-Manoa. Classes at UH-Manoa was way much harder than LCC classes. Plus, too, I would be working on campus. I wouldn't have the time to take care of Remie as well as Michael, especially when it came time to help with their homework. How would I be able to divide my time between two children's homework as well as my daily studying?

I spoke to Miguel a few times on the phone and in person. I was still scared of him, but he was changing slowly, becoming more religious and attending church events, according to Remie and Michael. Assuming that he was changing for the better, I thought it would be a good time to have Miguel take care of Michael.

Miguel didn't think it was a good idea at first. He thought it was best that both children stay with me. But I persisted, and eventually he relented, because he knew I would be too busy to tend to both children.

Michael moved to Mililani that during the summer of 1997.

Transferring to UH Manoa was a bit intimidating. The campus was twice as big as LCC, and there were thousands of new students being enrolled that winter semester. Luckily, I was able to get a job on campus in a department called Student, Equity, Excellence, and Diversity.

My co-workers were very nice and supportive, especially the director, Amy Agbayani. They helped me get settled in, as well as directed me to all the right places, offices, and classes that I needed to go. Agbayani always managed to guide me in the right direction. (At of the time of publication, Amy Agbayani retired as emeritus assistant vice chancellor of Student, Equity, Excellence and Diversity, and she still continues to help me whenever I reach out to her. Thank you, Amy.)

Some of my classes were in auditoriums or extra-big rooms where I felt small in the hundreds of students who were enrolled. I tried my best to fit in among the younger crowd, but there were a few who were like me: single parents striving to become self-sufficient and seeking higher education with the hope of obtaining a good-paying job.

I tried to live life one day at a time that first semester, however I still had a ghost to face from the past: post-traumatic stress. Whenever I talked to the counselors from the Counseling and Student Development Center regarding my terrible memories that Miguel put me through, I would cry and fall apart as if it had happened yesterday.

Falling Perfectly Without Trying

"Did this happen recently?" a counselor asked.

I tried to answer her through my tears. "No, it happened ten years ago."

"Not yesterday?" she asked, surprised.

"No."

"And how are your grades now?" she asked to change the subject, but it was clear she was very disturbed by my crying.

"I'm doing okay... I have three A's and one B as of now," I sniffled.

The semester would end in a week, so most students knew what their grades would be.

The staff realized that I was sick psychologically, and they tried to help me as much as they could. I experienced dissociative symptoms and felt detached from my body. A couple times, students and faculty near me realized I needed help and called the ambulance to bring me to the emergency room. I couldn't tell somedays if I was getting better or worse.

One day, a few months after the start of the semester during the fall, I became dissociated at home while Remie was at school. I knew I needed someone to come help me, because my mind wasn't all there. I was also depressed. I was scared to find out what I might do to myself. I called my sister, Deanna, and asked her to come to my apartment after she was finished with work.

In the time between hanging up the phone and Deanna and her husband, Dwayne, coming to my apartment, I opened a bottle of white wine and drank it all. I then went out on the lanai and sat on one of the plastic chairs I had put there to view the sunset.

All I could think about that day was that I wanted to end it all. I had failed as a mother and a student. I drank enough wine that I wouldn't feel anything if I took my life. I climbed over the railing of the lanai, but before I let go of the railing, Deanna and Dwayne came running into the apartment.

Dwayne rushed over and grabbed my arm. The next thing I knew, I had been thrown back onto the lanai and my sister was crying.

Once again, I was saved from myself. It could have ended tragically since my apartment was on the 11th floor.

A few times, I ended up in a closed unit at the hospital, because I needed immediate help by the psychiatric team. Once when I was there, I had a special visitor—former U.S. Congressman K. Mark Takai, who was a Hawai'i Representative at that time.

Takai found out I was there, and he was worried. He talked to me for a while and asked how he could help me, since he knew I was a student at UH Manoa.

Later after I was discharged, Mr. Takai helped me to be reunited with my daughter, who had been staying with my parents while I was in the hospital.

On three separate occasions within a month, I was admitted to the Kekela psychiatric unit at the Queen's Medical Center.

"This is where people like you can chill out for a couple of days," the doctor told me on one particular visit. But I knew what Kekela had to offer from my previous experience there five years earlier. Patients are evaluated by a psychiatrist to figure out the nature of their illness. Once they are evaluated, the doctors can treat them.

After a few days in Kekela, this same doctor said I had bi-polar disorder, which is a mental illness that has extreme lows (depression) and emotional highs (mania). Some of the things he offered to manage it were medication and therapy.

When he realized that I still wasn't getting better, he suggested ECT, or electroconvulsive therapy. Another name that's easy to identify it by is shock treatment.

"These treatments will keep you from being admitted to the hospital," the doctor said. "It's electronically-induced seizures, which is administered under anesthetic."

"I thought shock treatments are brutal," I said. "In the movies, shock treatments look terrible and scary."

The doctor rebuffed my thoughts on the subject. "No, shock treatments are not like what you see on television, where they make the procedure look worse than it really is. It's very quiet and is done to patients who are given anesthesia and a muscle relaxant. And, of course, you won't feel anything, because you'll be asleep."

I was reluctant, but eventually I agreed to it. I was desperate to feel better.

Later, I found out that electroconvulsive therapy is a treatment used in patients who have bipolar disorder or severe depression. ECT is especially used on patients who do not respond to other treatments and/or medications. It involves electrical stimulation of the brain while the patient is asleep from the anesthesia. Usually, a patient receives 2 to 3 ECT treatments for the first week, then the next couple of weeks once or twice per week for a total of 6 to 12 treatments. However, it all depends on the severity of the symptoms, and if the psychiatrists feel that the patient is responding to the treatment.

ECT treatments were first used in the 1940s. It has been recognized by the American Medical Association and the American Psychiatric Association, as well as the National Institute of Mental Health, as a safe treatment course. Over the past decades, the procedure has been improved greatly due to medical research.

Patients who have ECTs are associated with having a hard time learning new things, as well as having short-term memory loss. Some people may have trouble remembering events that happened weeks before the treatment. In most cases, after a few months passes after receiving ECTs, the patient's memory usually improves. Usually, but not always.

The side effects of ECT treatments may include fatigue, slight memory loss, nausea, confusion, or headaches. I received ECTs every other week for a couple months, and the treatment did keep me out of the hospital. However, there was a major side effect: I lost a chunk of my memory. I had to drop out of school during the spring semester because I couldn't study or retain what I was learning. After four months of ECTs, I told the doctor I'd had enough and didn't want to continue the treatments.

"It's affecting my memory," I said. "There was

a young woman who came up to me and asked if I remembered her, but I don't recall ever meeting her. She told me that I interviewed her for an article for UH-Manoa school's paper, but I don't remember her. I felt so bad, especially because she was a single parent."

Stopping the ECTs didn't solve anything. I couldn't concentrate, had short-term memory loss, and trouble retaining information, or understanding complex information while reading, leading to a sudden onset of academic troubles. I still suffered emotional and catastrophic reactions, and I feared their impact on my future.

Due to the state of my mind, my psychiatrist requested that a state-licensed psychologist do a neuropsychological evaluation on my brain to find out whether I was cognitively impaired, and to determine a baseline for the nature and the severity of my neuropsychological deficits.

I wanted to know if the situation with my memory was likely to be permanent or temporary. My whole livelihood depended on the analysis and evaluation of information. I needed to decide whether I was capable of returning to school.

It was determined that I had brain injury and would benefit from information from the Pacific Head Injury Association to maximize my strengths and overcome my deficits. The psychologist also said that more than likely I would not graduate with my bachelor's degree anytime soon. If I went back to school in the fall, I would need help from a tutor and need to request more time during test taking.

After a few weeks of thinking about their recommendations, I decided to continue school in the fall, despite all odds.

When school started, I worked twice as hard to keep up my grades. I recorded all my classes during lectures, then reviewed and rewrote my notes before every class. I requested the help of tutors and cut my course load to three classes. I resumed appointments with the counselor at the Counseling and Student Development Center to help with my post-traumatic stress.

As the months went by, the crying episodes lessened when I had flashbacks of what Miguel had done to me. Whenever I had to talk about the past, it no longer seemed like it happened just yesterday, which was a relief both to myself and the staff in the counseling office.

In my writing classes that semester, I did extremely well. To fulfill the math requirement, I was able to take a philosophy class instead, which helped a great deal. I continued to work part-time on campus, as well as handle all the challenges of being a single mother living alone with my daughter a few blocks from the university, and barely seeing my son.

***

Remie attended Kaimuki High School, less than a mile away from our apartment complex. I tried to make a wonderful life for her by showering her with things that teen girls dreamed of—designer jeans, blouses, coach bags, and numerous pairs of shoes. However, Remie

Falling Perfectly Without Trying

needed supervision and more time with me than I had to spare. I was busy with my class assignments, my campus job, and writing for the *Ka Leo* newspaper.

I kept a schedule of all the things I needed to do each day, and balancing it was extremely hard. Sometimes things didn't go as expected, which resulted in me spending even less time with Remie and not being able to give her the attention she truly needed. We had some fun times together, but most of the time our relationship was strained.

While I attended UH-Manoa, I found myself becoming a spokesperson for welfare recipients and single parents. I'd speak at meetings, large events, a few times at the State Capitol, and at conventions. One of the events was a retirement for Dr. Doris Ching, who at the time was the UH Vice President for Student Affairs.

Dr. Ching had been very helpful while I attended UH Manoa. She was a very sympathetic and open-hearted person not only to me, but to everyone she met. I'm thankful I got to know her. (At the time of publication, she is Emeritus Vice President for Student Affairs, University of Hawaii System).

The government dismantled the JOBS program, and laws for welfare benefits began changing. As a result, many students on welfare had to drop out of school and go to work full-time. It was unrealistic for many of them to continue with school, especially since their children needed them. A few made it to graduation, and it was for those able to "stick it out" that I spoke for at numerous events.

Jenny Duhaylonsod Delos Santos

During my final year of school, I had accomplished a great deal with work, school, and writing for *Ka Leo*. Because I had written so many articles, the newspaper editors let me write about subjects that I was interested in.

I had reached my ultimate dream…to be a reporter for a newspaper. I remembered making that my long-term goal while attending Leeward Community College, but I hadn't specified what newspaper. That didn't matter. I had accomplished what I wanted to do, and the *Ka Leo* staff honored me as "Best News Reporter of the Year" my senior year.

Another achievement was overcoming post-traumatic stress disorder. Thanks to the help of my counselor, I was able to control my nightmares and terrifying memories. My PTSD didn't entirely go away, but it became manageable and not as frightening.

That summer, I walked across the huge stage and received my bachelors of arts degree in journalism. It was a very proud moment for me, especially since it had taken almost a decade to achieve.

By graduating, I thought I had it made. I thought I could go anywhere and people would want to hire me. I didn't know that trying to get a job would be another nightmare. I went to numerous interviews and always came up empty-handed.

As a result, I started drinking a lot. During my college days, I drank several times a week due to stress, but drinking became a daily occurrence after graduation. I would buy numerous bottles of wine and drink until I got drunk. Instead of feeling good inside,

I got depressed.

This didn't help the relationship between Remie and I. I wasn't the best influence. However, I tried the best I could for my daughter at the time. I provided a place for her to live, food, gave her money to buy clothes and encouraged her to go to school every weekday.

After several months of searching for a job and living on next to nothing, I went to an employment agency. The search took such a long time, I got impatient, desperate as I waited for a writing position to come up. The agency asked if I would take any office job instead, and I agreed. A few days later, I went to an interview at an accounting firm, and the staff liked me immediately. I was hired the same day and started there shortly after.

I was happy to get a job, but I felt like I had failed. My dream of working in the media industry had been shattered. Imagine, years and years of practicing at being a reporter at the LCC and UH-Manoa newspapers as well as the *Fil-Am Courier*, then to end up in a totally different industry. It crushed me. It was an extremely sad moment in my life.

To make matters worse, the Department of Human Services had cut off my food stamps, medical benefits, and other financial assistance due to the income I was receiving. That income wasn't enough for Remie and I to continue living in our apartment, so we moved back to 'Ewa Beach, where the rent was much more affordable. We would be closer to family, who were willing to help us. But new challenges lie ahead.

Chapter Six
Dreaming Big, But Failing, Too

While Remie was at her grandmother's house in 'Ewa Beach one day, I was at our old apartment in Honolulu, trying to pack up all our belongings.

As I was wiping down all the countertops in the kitchen, I couldn't help feeling like I had failed. I was depressed. The more I thought that I had failed, the more I headed toward wanting to commit suicide.

Without hesitating, I grabbed a bottle of medication — 800 milligrams in each tablet — out of the medicine cabinet and put it on the kitchen counter. I took out an opened bottle of white wine from the refrigerator and put it beside it. I counted thirty pills, put ten in my mouth and drank them down with a couple gulps of wine. I put another ten pills in my mouth and drank more wine, then put the last ten in my mouth and swallowed them with the rest of the wine.

Afterward, I sat at the kitchen table and waited for it to take effect. While the minutes passed, so many thoughts went through my mind. One of which was that the medicine and wine wasn't working as fast as I'd hope it would. I began thinking about my children

Falling Perfectly Without Trying

and hoping they would be okay. They were both in high school now. I thought about Mom, Dad and my siblings, and their families. I started to wonder if it was the right thing to do—to end it all.

I decided to call my sister, Bertha, to say good-bye.

I wasn't making any sense as I continued to talk to her over the phone.

Bertha became suspicious, knowing my state of mind the past couple of days.

"Jenny, what did you take?" she asked. "Did you swallow medicine? Are you okay?"

After a few moments of not answering her, my sister called 9-1-1. Minutes later, the emergency medical technicians arrived at the apartment and found me unconscious on the floor on a blanket.

They tried to wake me up, but I wasn't responding.

They put an IV into my arm, then put me on a stretcher and rushed me downstairs into the ambulance.

While sleeping, I dreamt that I was a reporter for a local news station, got sick, and died. When the news anchors went on the air the day I died, they announced that they had lost one of their fellow reporters. The dream was so sad and seemed so real.

When I finally opened my eyes, Deanna and a doctor were hovering over me.

"She's awake!" the doctor said in relief. "She's going to be okay."

"Where am I?" I asked quietly, trying to sit up in the hospital bed.

"In the hospital," Deanna answered, all the love evident in her voice and eyes. She was relieved to see that her big sister had survived the ordeal. "I'm so glad you're okay, Jenny. I love you so much."

After six hours, the ER doctors reluctantly let me go home under Deanna's supervision. Deanna and Dwayne and I got into their SUV and drove back to 'Ewa Beach.

When we got to my parents' home, I got out of the car and went into the house.

"Are you okay?" Mom asked.

"Yeah...I'm okay. Just really tired."

I sat on the couch in the living room as Remie walked in from the hallway.

"Mommy," Remie said. "You're home. But, you don't look too good."

"I'm fine, Remie," I said. "Just tired."

"Jenny, why don't you sleep in the bedroom," Mom said, concern in her voice. "Maybe you'll feel better."

I got up from the couch, slowly walked through the hallway and into the bedroom, where there were two twin beds with beige yellow comforters. I sat on the bed next to the window and lay down. Then I fell into a deep sleep.

The next day, my sister Bertha dropped me off to see my social worker at his office in Kalihi. I still wasn't feeling well, so I curled up on the carpet while leaning against the file cabinets.

He suggested I see a psychiatrist who worked in the same building, and the doctor gave me a prescription for thirty sleeping pills. I'm guessing they probably thought I needed something to sedate myself since I was so depressed.

Falling Perfectly Without Trying

We went to fill the prescription at the nearest pharmacy store. As soon as I got the bottle, I took one pill. When I got in the car, I took one pill after another. He never saw me taking all the pills, but he was deeply concerned about my well-being. He knew I was in no condition to travel back to 'Ewa Beach by myself on the city Bus. So, he drove me all the way back to my parents' house in Ewa' Beach.

When I got home, I retreated to my bedroom and took the rest of the pills and then fell into a deep sleep.

My family grew worried because I slept so long. I barely responded when they tried to wake me up. They did not know that I had swallowed all thirty pills. As a result, they took me back to the hospital, where I was again admitted to Kekela. All I really did was sleep for four days, and I barely spoke to anyone.

While I was in the hospital, my family called the accounting firm where I was employed and told them I wouldn't be returning to work. Mom realized I was too devastated at being a "failure" due to working at the accounting firm and not in the media industry like I had always dreamed.

After I spoke with the psychologist and psychiatrist at Kekela, they realized I was an alcoholic and had been for a couple of years. I was drinking a bottle of wine daily to escape all of the stress. Prior to being discharged, the doctors ordered me to go to outpatient classes to help me stop drinking. The classes were Monday to Friday and lasted for four months.

When I started the outpatient classes at the hospital, I met a lot of people who drank alcohol or took drugs.

Jenny Duhaylonsod Delos Santos

At first, I was very quiet and shy. I became friends with many of them, especially those who were my age. We were in a small support group, trying to encourage each other to stop drinking and/or using drugs.

I began attending Alcoholic Anonymous meetings, which were held at different locations every day. Those attending the meetings came from different backgrounds and locations. Some worked, and used their lunch hour to attend the meetings.

I became good friends with the members, and their support helped a great deal after the outpatient classes at the hospital ended. The best part of the AA meetings was that the attendees would share their hopes and dreams as well as challenges and tribulations. I realized we were all so much alike, and we all had a common goal…to stop drinking.

A year passed. I finally felt better about myself and had a much better attitude about life. One day on the grounds of the Queen's Medical Center, I met an old school friend from college, Yolanda, who worked for a daily newspaper in Honolulu.

"Jenny, there's an opening at the newspaper. Why don't you try to apply for it?" Yolanda asked.

"I don't know if I should," I said. "I haven't worked for a while."

"At least try, please. I'll put in a good word for you," she said.

After much discussion with my family, I decided to go to the newspaper office and apply. I was so scared.

When I got to the *Honolulu Star-Bulletin* newsroom, I met a person by the name of MaryJane. She said there

Falling Perfectly Without Trying

was a clerk dispatcher's position open, but I needed to have a driver's license.

"I'm sorry, MaryJane, but I don't have a driver's license," I explained.

"Do you think that you can get your license in a couple of days?"

I shook my head and made a sad face. "I don't know. I can try."

"Well, let me take your typing test first, then we can discuss it more," she said.

She gave me the typing test. I passed it with a 100% accuracy rate, which made her happy.

"Why don't you take the driver's test soon, and call me as soon as you pass it," MaryJane said.

I agreed reluctantly.

I went home and explained the dilemma to Deanna and Dwayne.

"I can teach you to drive, Jenny," Dwayne volunteered.

"Are you sure you have time?" I asked.

"Yes," Dwayne said. "I can start teaching you tomorrow."

When the next day came, I had cold feet. I was too scared, and told Deanna and Dwayne the truth.

I called MaryJane at the newsroom and told her that I couldn't take the driver's test, but I didn't tell her why. She expressed her disappointment, but told me that maybe there will be other positions open in the future.

It was the month of November, and the State Capitol was hiring for next year's legislation team. I went to visit Rep. K. Mark Takai and asked if his office had any openings.

"Yes, we do have openings," Takai answered. "Why don't you go downstairs to the basement and get an application so you can apply?"

I started working for Takai on Jan. 3rd as a legislative aide. It was very exciting and tiring at the same time, however, I liked working there.

On April 20, I saw Yolanda at the State Capitol.

"Jenny, there's another clerk opening at the newspaper again," Yolanda said excitedly. "Why don't you apply?"

I was worried. "I'm not sure if I should."

"Just try. I'll put a good word in for you."

As a result, I went to the newsroom at Restaurant Row and turned my resume application in to the first person I saw in the newsroom of the newspaper.

Two days later, I received a call from the newsroom's office manager. They wanted to interview me.

When I went home that afternoon, I ran into Mom, who was cooking dinner.

"Wow! I can't believe it, Mom!" I said in amazement. "My dream of working for a newspaper might come true."

"That's great, Jenny. But you have to go through the interview first," Mom said.

"Yes. I better find out what I'm going to wear. It's so exciting!" I said.

I decided on a black pencil silhouette skirt with a matching jacket that had a double fold-over collar and long sleeves. To finish off the outfit, I wore tan nylon stockings and a black Coach shoulder bag.

"You look very professional, Jenny!" Mom and Deanna both said when I came out of the bedroom on the day of the interview.

"You will surely get the job," Deanna said.

"Pray on it," Mom told me. "With God, anything is possible."

In the interview, the office manager asked me a few simple questions and told me I was hired. I thought all my problems were solved, and that Michael, Remie, and I would live happily ever after. I went to the Bus stop and caught the Bus to 'Ewa Beach and went directly to see Mom.

"Mom, Mom! I got the job!" I said as I jumped up and down with happiness. "Imagine, they hired me!"

Mom was stunned and couldn't believe it.

"See, when you leave it up to the Lord?" Mom said. "He answers your prayers."

"Yes! My dream came true. The newspaper hired me. I'm so so so HAPPY!"

I finally calmed down a few days later and realized I had other things to address. One of the most important was Remie, who had suffered a lot through the years.

Because I tended to my own problems of school, work, and trying to become self-sufficient so I didn't have to rely on government help, Remie was left at home alone many times when she was in middle and high school. Because I lived so far from my family while going to school, I couldn't depend on my parents or siblings to care for Remie when I was not at home. She'd cook rice and open canned goods when she was hungry. When I came home from work or school, I would find the house in disarray and cooked food strewn over the counters. Knowing full well that Remie was unsupervised, I usually didn't get mad, but I did feel terrible inside. I just didn't know what else to do.

In school, Remie had a hard time. She had a learning disability that prevented her from reading or writing clear sentences. Since I wasn't at home much, I wasn't able to help her. It was difficult for Remie to study and do her homework. When she reached her senior year, her teachers at the high school tried to help her, but it was too late. I wasn't sure how she pulled it off, but she graduated her senior year with a diploma. Instead of feeling elated, I felt like the school had failed her and that I had contributed to her failure.

Soon after Remie had graduated, we found out that she suffered from severe depression. Her therapist said one of the reasons she was suffering was that she had to stay home alone when she was young.

"Jenny, you tried the best you could while you were in school," the therapist said. "You can't blame yourself for her illness. Plus, she's also having flashbacks from when your husband was abusing you. It's like she's having post-traumatic stress.

The past is the past, and you can't change what has happened. And you can't go on blaming yourself and consistently make up for what happened. It's not healthy to keep on giving and helping her all the time. It's not good for her. Instead of helping her, you are enabling Remie and making her depend on you for everything, which is bad. What's going to happen to

Falling Perfectly Without Trying

her if something happens to you?"

I didn't know. I had tried to talk to Remie about the future and encourage her to be fully independent. However, as her mom, I felt like it was my responsibility to look after her despite what our therapists said.

Miguel hadn't spoken to Remie for many years and didn't understand that she wasn't well. He thought that God had healed our daughter, so she must be okay. He also believed that she didn't need psychiatric help, medicine, or assistance.

We experienced many challenges and setbacks during Remie's illness. She moved out of her apartment without telling me or our family, stopped her food stamps without consulting me, and cut off all her hair because of stress.

When Remie did find a job, which usually was at a fast-food restaurant, she wasn't able to handle the stress that came from the other employees training her. Nor was she able to complete her job requirements, including taking customer's orders. Often, I had to leave my own job to console her and prevent her from committing suicide.

At one time, Remie dated an ex-con who had a history of multiple arrests and convictions. She first met the guy at a nearby store. One night, he followed her home. He found a way into our secured building in the early morning hours, and people started getting suspicious. The police came, and six officers tackled him to the ground. It really shook up Remie and me, because we had never experienced policemen trying to arrest someone.

But no matter what happened, I was always there for her while others wouldn't do anything to help her. I wouldn't abandon my daughter.

One day, Remie and I were at a Starbucks in downtown Honolulu, and we talked about the past. I rarely spoke to her about it, and at first, I was afraid to talk about such a sensitive topic. I didn't want her to hate Miguel for what he did to me. However, I really wanted to know how she felt and what she remembered. I asked her if she remembered the guns he used and her father yelling and threatening me, or how badly Miguel treated her and her brother. She said she remembered a little.

"I remember seeing a gun on the dresser in the bedroom and you crying," Remie said. "I also remember Dad picking me up and putting me outside of the apartment when it was raining."

While we talked about how her father abused me, Remie said, "Mom, I know why you never got hit from my father. You never fought back. A couple of years ago, he and I got into a terrible argument, so I hit him. He hit me back really hard. He didn't leave a mark, but it hurt."

I was stunned. I never knew about that confrontation between them. She had never hinted about it, not even once to me.

We talked about Michael's relationship with Miguel. I worried about him all the time.

When we lived in California, the children were usually asleep when Miguel threatened me. However, Michael was older than Remie, and he could have been awake during those terrifying nights. Through the years, I wondered about how much the past had affected Michael, too.

When Michael lived with Miguel, he tried to teach Michael how to drive. Remie said that their father would always yell at Michael during the lessons, as he used to do with me. As a result, Michael had a difficult time learning to drive. He eventually gave up. He uses the Bus to get around.

Whenever I called Michael on the landline at his dad's house, he was always in a rush and tried to end the call. Like as if, he was afraid to talk to me.

When Remie and I are with him, Michael doesn't talk very much. He prefers to be alone and tells us that he has to be somewhere else. It's sad how one person could hurt three people in his family so much.

I find Michael's behavior strange, and I often wonder if the past has gotten to him, too.

Chapter Seven
The Reality of Cancer

During the months of June and July 2015, I was faced with another huge challenge that unexpectedly hit me.

I met with my insurance agent, who encouraged me to get a mammogram so I could put in a claim for a free $100.

So on June 25th, I went for a mammogram. It was an annual testing that I usually take once every year. When I went to work after the appointment, I went to my insurance's website, got the claim application, and filled it out. The next day while I was out shopping, a nurse called me and told me I needed to take more tests, mammograms, and an ultrasound as soon as possible.

I became worried. So many thoughts ran through my head.

What if I really had cancer?

Mom had died of cancer in 2006. What if I had cancer and died, too? What would happen to Remie and Michael? How would they feel?

For the next couple of weeks, I was on an emotional roller coaster. I had so many appointments with various departments at the Queen's Medical Center and was taking all kinds of tests, but no one could tell me the results. I was told that I had to wait and wait and wait some more. I was worried and anxious.

All kinds of questions were going through my mind, and it was really affecting me at work. Luckily, my co-workers were supportive and understanding, otherwise I wouldn't have been able to go through those dark days of waiting.

Finally, just before July ended, I met with my internist and he said I had the beginning of cancer in my breast. He referred me to a cancer surgeon whose office was right next to his.

When I had the chance to speak with the surgeon, she confirmed with me that I had DCIS, ductal carcinoma in situ.

"Your cancer is really small and in the early stages, Jenny. It isn't life threatening," the doctor said. "But in any case, it is cancer. No doubt about that. All you have to do is have an operation to take out the cells as well as go through five to six weeks of radiation."

I told her that I had a lot of relatives who had cancer, including Mom, who had lung and breast cancer. She recommended that I see a genetics doctor.

When I tried to make an appointment to see the genetics doctor, I was told that I had to wait eighteen days for approval from my insurer—another long waiting period. I finally came to terms with the fact that I would get the results *someday*...so I stopped being anxious and impatient about it. Cancer was apparently a hurry up and wait game.

After waiting a little more than two weeks, the Genetics Department called me. I was given an appointment with a genetics counselor. When we met, the counselor went into great detail about who in my family previously had cancer as well as what was BRCA I and BRCA II.

From what I understood, BRCA I and BRCA II were human genes that could produce tumor suppressor proteins that helped repair damaged DNA and ensure the stability of cells' genetic material. When these genes were altered or mutated, the body may not be able to properly repair DNA damage. Therefore, the cells may develop additional genetic alterations that could lead to cancer. Specific mutations that were inherited in BRCA I and BRCA II may increase the risk of ovarian and breast cancer, which had been associated with risks that could lead to other types of cancer.

After finishing my family tree from the history I gave her, the counselor felt I would benefit from taking the Myriad myRisk hereditary cancer test. If the result came out negative, then there would be nothing to worry about, according to a booklet that she gave me to read.

"Because of this, your risk for a hereditary cancer is lower, but not completely ruled out."

She went to explain that if the test comes out positive, there would be other tests to perform, and a mastectomy of both breasts would also be recommended.

With my heart beating wildly, I decided to go through with the test, which she administered that same day. She said I had to wait a few days for the results. Yet,

Falling Perfectly Without Trying

another waiting period to go through.

I had just come home from the hospital from a diabetic appointment when I received a call from the Genetics Department.

"Jenny, the results are in," the nurse said. "Can you come in today at 2:30 PM?"

My immediate thought was that it was bad news, and my mind was thinking the worst scenario. Questions kept going through my head as I started to panic.

Why would they call me in so fast?
What if I had to have a mastectomy?

I told the nurse that I could come in. In a short while, I was back at the hospital that I had just left.

I sat in the Genetics Department waiting to hear the worst. Many negative thoughts ran through my mind. Finally, the nurse called me in, and I met the counselor in her office.

"Jenny, the results came back negative," she said. "You don't have BRCA I or BRCA II."

I looked up at her with surprise. I couldn't believe it. I had imagined the worst.

"Did you expect bad news?"

"I thought the test was going to be positive and that I would need to have a mastectomy," I said. "I was so worried."

After much explaining, the counselor said I could talk to my surgeon. I wasted no time and went straight to the surgeon's office. Thankfully, the receptionist said the doctor could see me that day.

We discussed three options:

Go through with the operation and take out the cancer. See if it had become invasive. If it had, go through a second operation and have a mastectomy. But if it is still non-invasive, then just go through radiation.

Have a mastectomy only on the right side.

Have a mastectomy on both sides.

I decided to take the first option and agreed to go through surgery, then radiation if everything worked out. I already knew I couldn't imagine having a mastectomy on my right breast, let alone on both breasts.

I was scared, but certain that I made the right decision. I was worried about not waking up after the surgery, but they assured me that it would be fast and quick.

My husband, Pancho followed me into the surgery prep room, along with my cousin Peggy, who I was surprised to see. I couldn't figure out how she discovered that I would be having surgery that day.

Later, I learned that my sister had told Peggy a couple days previously about my surgery. It was a relief having Pancho and Peggy there, because I was still scared and unsure what would happen, despite the doctor's assurances that it would be quick.

A few days later, my doctor advised me to go to the Radiation Therapy Department in a month, after the surgery area had healed some.

Despite my ordeal, I decided to return to work two days later. I didn't want to take off more days than I needed to since I had no sick days remaining and only had two vacation days left for the rest of the year. Plus, I was told I could return to work right away.

When I showed up at work, everyone was speechless. They couldn't believe that I was okay.

A month later, I returned to the hospital and spoke to the doctor in the Radiation Department. She said, "Since you opted for radiation instead of having a mastectomy, you will have to undergo five weeks of radiation therapy. You'll have to come here every weekday for five weeks."

"Every weekday," I repeated, feeling nauseated. "Wow...that's a long time."

"You won't feel tired or get nauseated during radiation treatments," she said.

However, before I began treatment, I started to worry again. The thought of going to the hospital every weekday seemed overwhelming. In addition, my entire schedule and all my other activities would have to revolve around these radiation appointments. It all sounded so complicated.

What if I got nauseated?

What if I lost my hair?

What did it really mean to get radiation?

What if I got tired? Would I be able to go to work afterward? Oh my goodness...what would I do?

On my first treatment day, my anxiety and stress were sky-high. While I sat in the waiting room, I noticed the other patients around me in hospital gowns and robes. Employees in hospital scrubs came through a door and called people's names every fifteen minutes. One by one, the patients followed the employees through the door. By the time a woman in a long white coat called my name, I was edgy and anxious. She introduced herself.

"You don't have to worry," she assured me. "You won't feel a thing. It doesn't hurt. All you have to do is lie on the flatbed, and we'll do the rest."

She said she was a radiation technician. She introduced me to another technician.

"It's mandatory that we have the patients tell us their birth date every time they go into the room," she said. "It's for security reasons. When is your birthday?"

After I did so, I realized I'd have radiation on my birthday. That seemed so sad for me to have to deal with cancer on my birthday.

While one technician helped me off the flatbed, the other one said, "Usually people are so scared the first time that they have an anxiety attack. You did great!"

"Wow," I exclaimed. "I'm glad I didn't get that scared."

"Next time, it'll be faster. The whole ordeal takes about fifteen minutes."

As the days and weeks passed by, I got used to the routine. Every weekday I would get up around 6:30 AM, then take a shower and get ready. By the time 8 AM came, I was headed out the door of my apartment. Then I would catch the Bus.

What made the days a lot brighter was the radiation technicians, who were all nice. They were always in good spirits and had something interesting to say. Many times, they asked about the newspaper and my job.

As my five weeks of radiation were coming to an end,

Falling Perfectly Without Trying

I realized that soon I wouldn't see the radiation team anymore. I had grown very fond of them, especially since they were so positive and seemed so upbeat. The thought saddened me.

On my birthday, the technicians all sang *Happy Birthday* to me. I was so grateful. I wanted to do something special for each of them in return.

For the men, I got candies with a plague that had an inspirational quote. For the one female technician, I picked up scented bath salts and lotions. They had made my twenty-five days of radiation so much brighter.

Pancho came with me one day, and he enjoyed speaking to the radiation technicians.

"Yes, they are really nice," Pancho said. "It makes a whole lot of difference that they are nice to the patients, because then the patients will have a positive experience rather than dreading the therapy."

"I don't think I would've made it this long if it wasn't for their kindness and hospitality," I said.

On Thursday, Nov. 12, was my last day of radiation. I had mixed feelings. I was glad the therapy was over, but I was sad I would not see the technicians again. As a result, I was teary-eyed as I said goodbye that day.

As I stood outside the hospital, I realized that I had reached the end of another chapter in my life. While I fell perfectly without trying, I never saw the cancer coming. I got up and walked on with life despite the odds once again.

Chapter Eight
Searching for HAPPYNESS

Sometimes I wonder what would've happened if I had taken another route. For instance, if I hadn't finished college and graduated with my associate's degree instead. Maybe, I would have brought up both of my children on my own. Would life have been better or worse? Would we all be living together rather than living miles apart from one another like we are now? Would we be just making ends meet with me having a minimum-paying job?

Would my kids have been better psychologically and able to handle all the challenges that would come their way? Would they have known what it is like to achieve goals and dreams? Would they have become successful in their own way?

There are so many "what ifs" and sometimes, I get really sad thinking about it all.

It seems I have failed as a mother. I was so focused on myself and trying to do well in school and to reach my own dreams. Trying to stay healthy. Now, I look at my past and I feel like they were suffering because of me. At the time of publication, Michael is a professional college student studying whatever trips his fancy, and Remie is unable to hold a job, let alone be able to live with other people under the same roof.

However, there were a few successes with my children. For one thing, they are both healthy and live in a safe environment. Michael lives with his father's family, which includes his grandma, two uncles and his father. Remie has a place of her own in Kalihi, located close to downtown Honolulu.

On top of that, Michael and Remie are drug-free and don't smoke. They also don't have any medical issues, such as diabetes and cancer.

Even though I didn't give Michael and Remie my full attention when they were in grade school and high school, they both came out pretty good.

***

As for my own journey while being a student at LCC and UH Manoa, I met countless students, faculty, staff and administrators, who all helped shape me to what I am today.

I had the opportunity to work in the office of Rep. Mark Takai at the Hawai'i State Capitol during the 1990s. With a lot of patience and guidance, Takai and his staff helped me to understand politics and how bills were passed. One of the bills that I was instrumental in helping to pass was the bill that would allow a student to become a voting member on the University of Hawai'i Board of Regents. It didn't pass both the House and the Senate right away; however, I learned what it took to pass a bill as well as the process that a bill must go through.

The best thing about working in Takai's office was that I was treated with kindness, and I felt like part of a big family—*ohana*). I worked for Takai for a total of two years as a student intern and then two years as a legislative aide.

As life took us in different directions, Takai eventually served in the United States House of Representatives in Washington D.C., which he represented Hawai'i's first congressional district. He passed away on July 20, 2016.

During the summer of 2000, I had the opportunity to take a UH-Manoa class taught in the Philippines by UH professor Dean Alegado. Seven other students from across the United States took part in the journey, which brought us to different areas of the Philippines. It may be considered a third-world country by many, but we saw beautiful lands and castles. Once we even were served a whole roast pig (lechon) on a huge table, fit for royalty. It was a wonderful experience to visit the hometown of my ancestors, and I finally felt proud to be a Filipina.

So much has happened over the course of twenty-eight years that it's hard to imagine what life would've been like if I had not had the courage to leave Miguel and return to O'ahu with my children in 1987.

Goals, dreams, and perseverance are what got me where I am today. Would I have wanted anything less than what I have now?

Falling Perfectly Without Trying

***

I got to know Pancho while writing for a Filipino newspaper, FilAm Courier, in the summer of 1997. His cousin owned the newspaper, and we were introduced to each other when he came to visit one day.

When I transferred to UH Manoa in the Fall of 1997, he worked at the Outreach program. Pancho and I met again while I was writing an investigative article for the school newspaper. We dated for many years.

Originally, Pancho is from a town called Kahului, located on the island of Maui. Most of Pancho's family lived in Kahului. We traveled to Maui about two or three times a month, especially when his mom got really sick.

There were two airlines that traveled inter-island, but we always made arrangements to travel on one of them.

We looked forward to going to Maui, and we traveled so much that we were able to relax in the lounge of the airlines prior to boarding the plane.

When the weekend was over, we bought omiyage for all our friends and co-workers on O'ahu. Sometimes we bought mochi; however, when Krispie Kreme opened a store on Maui, bringing donuts from Krispie Kreme to O'ahu was the highlight of the trip. Our friends and co-workers would get so excited when we brought back omiyage.

On November 3, 2007, we married. It was twenty years after I left my first husband, which was in September 1987.

Jenny Duhaylonsod Delos Santos

Because it was Pancho's first wedding, I agreed to have the wedding ceremony and reception on Maui. We wanted to make sure that Pancho's relatives could all make it to the ceremony and reception.

My relatives, co-workers, and friends from O'ahu were able to come and enjoy the festivities with us. All-in-all, there were a total of 400 guests at the ceremony and reception. It was such a beautiful occasion.

My seven bridesmaids, two flower girls and I got ready at Pancho's brother's two-story home. It was so exciting to be all together and have professional hair dressers fix our hair as well as put make-up on all of us. To top it off, his brother's home was extremely beautiful. It was like being in a five-star hotel.

When it was time, three limousine cars brought us to the church where Pancho and I would be married. At the church, we met up with the seven groomsmen, the ring bearer, Pancho and all the guests. It was such a memorable event.

After taking numerous pictures with the bridal party, we somehow made it to the reception where the guests were enjoying the entertainment.

One of the highlights of the reception was the "money dance," which is a Filipino culture tradition. The guests would come up to the bride and groom, while they are dancing to a slow song. Each of the guests would put a napkin around a folded dollar bill and put it on the bride and groom's lips. Then the bride or groom would spit out the napkin (with the dollar bill folded inside) unto the floor, where the bridesmaids would pick up each bill and put it in a small basket.

Falling Perfectly Without Trying

The money dance is a fun activity at wedding receptions, and it can last until all the guests are finished giving money to the bride and groom. While this custom is a great way for the guests to contribute a little extra cash to the newlyweds, it also shows good fortune in togetherness for the bride and groom.

Overall, I was overwhelmed by how well everything turned out, because it was nothing like my first wedding. It was everything a person could ever dream of and more.

Despite being so dazzled at the wedding, getting married again was a hard decision to make. I remembered all the abuse I went through with my first husband. Part of me feared life would repeat itself all over again.

It hasn't.

Pancho treats me very well, and he and I are still married ten years later. Yes, we do have our ups and downs as well as challenges, but our relationship is nothing like my first marriage. He also gets along well with my children and my family. Mom would totally approve.

I've been working at the newspaper for thirteen years now, but I'm still paying for my student loans. I live from paycheck to paycheck. I thought if I went back to school and got another degree, then I could find a higher-paying job so I wouldn't have to worry about finances so much.

I enrolled in 2014 at Heald College to pursue an associate's in business administration. I went to classes at night after finishing work. It was challenging but rewarding. I did so well that I was invited to join Phi Theta Kappa at Heald, and I worked on their newsletter, which thrilled me.

However, two of my required subjects were payroll and accounting. I realized I had hit a brick wall. I wasn't good in math, so I struggled in classes that involved math. I became emotional because of that. In addition, Remie was having a lot of trouble again. I knew I had to decide whether to continue with college or drop out. Being in school was very positive for me, and it was a difficult choice to make. I held out until the very end of the quarter, but when school started again in June 2015, I didn't return. I had to say good-bye to everyone who was close to me. It was heartbreaking, but my daughter's well-being is more important than a degree.

That same month, Chris Gardner, author of *The Pursuit of Happyness*, came to town. The movie based on his book was also going to be shown. I loved the movie; therefore, I arranged my schedule so Remie and I would be able to attend Gardner's talk that evening.

After the movie, Gardner took questions from the audience. I wanted to say something, but I was too nervous. Afterwards, he stayed by the stage and spoke to whoever wanted to meet him. Remie and I stood in the long line and when it was our turn, I introduced my daughter and myself.

"I was a single parent for twenty years, and I feel like I haven't succeeded because we are not wealthy," I told Mr. Gardner as tears slipped down my cheeks.

"But you are both here," Mr. Gardner said. "You have to redefine what success is. It doesn't always mean that you must be rich. You have succeeded because you came this far, and you're both here."

He then gave both of us a big hug.

I had to really think about what he said. After pondering and reflecting for a couple of days, I came to terms with the fact that I'm not rich, but I am successful in that I reached my dreams and my children are both healthy and safe.

***

Since I've been on my own journey in the "Pursuit of Happyness," I can now say that I'm comfortable with my life. I realize that a person can make adjustments in life in order to be fulfilled and happy.

While I attended Heald, I had two goals aside from obtaining another degree. One goal had to do with someone I met at Heald. Primo Castro was the head of Student Services, and he was able to speak in front of all the students without looking at notes. His speeches so inspired me that I wanted to know how he learned to speak in front of a large crowd with so much enthusiasm. I later found out that he was a member of Toastmasters, and he won many awards for speaking. My goal was to get involved with Toastmasters, and also be able to speak in front of people without notes.

In the middle of June 2015, I joined the Toastmasters-Waterfront Plaza Chapter, and they held meetings at Waterfront Plaza in downtown Honolulu. Two weeks later, I did my first speech called "Leaving for a Better Life," and I was a nervous wreck! What if I forgot my lines, even though I spent so much time memorizing them? What if the other members wouldn't accept me for who I was? I would be revealing so many things about myself in the speech, including going through domestic abuse, having post-traumatic stress, and being an alcoholic.

I stumbled over a few words, forgot a sentence or two, and said too many "ums" and "ands." Plus, I was sweating and had symptoms of anxiety. Overall, I think I did okay, because the members came up to me and said it was a good speech.

What I didn't expect was that after the meeting, a longtime member of Toastmasters, Caroline Kunitake, came up to me.

"I was very impressed with your speech," she said. "I think you should enter the Toastmasters International Contest next year."

I was stunned and couldn't believe what I just heard.

For the next few days, she told me everything I needed to know to prepare for the contest. The event would also help me realize another dream of mine, which is to someday go to Washington, D.C. By luck, next year's Toastmasters International Contest would be in Washington, D.C. Wow!

I always wanted to go to Washington, D.C., and I will finally have a chance to go. To top it off, I would be able to visit U.S. Congressman Mark Takai in Washington, D.C. I was so happy that my goals might come true.

"Yes, I will compete in the contest, and I promise I will work hard for a whole year," I told Caroline.

Falling Perfectly Without Trying

I was on my way to reaching another goal and dream.

***

With Caroline's help, I spoke at a women's support group in July 2015 at the Institute of Human Services, a homeless shelter in Honolulu. Even though I practiced and practiced, I was still nervous. I wrote out my speech on multicolored index cards, which I used when I appeared before the support group at IHS.

The women's support group welcomed me with a lot of enthusiasm. After my talk, each of the 15 women who were present gave their own short speech, telling me that mine was very good and that they hoped I would prosper in Toastmasters. I was a bit overwhelmed and surprised at what they told me, especially because I thought that I was the one who should be giving positive input to them. I had my own house and belongings, while they all lived at IHS and barely owned anything. Yet, compliments were coming to me.

Besides my speech, I also had prepared goodie bags for each of the women which contained makeup items and candies, as well as poems and domestic abuse fliers and pamphlets. I handed out the bags just before leaving, along with much praise, smiles, and gratitude. Many of them gave me warm hugs and kisses. They were filled with so much love, which blew me away, considering the life they were living at the moment.

The visit to IHS was so heartwarming. I felt really good inside.

Two weeks later, I received a nice gift from the

women's support group, which surprised me a great deal. Imagine, the women barely had anything, but they were still able to buy me a thank-you card and a book, "Soul Healing Miracles" by Dr. and Master Zhi Gang Sha. I hadn't realized that I had made such a big impact on them. Hopefully, I will meet them again sometime under better circumstances.

Over the next several months, I gave about six speeches for Toastmasters. In one of the bigger events, I was a featured speaker for the District 49 Toastmasters Evaluation Contest in September 2015.

My heart was racing, butterflies were in my stomach, and my hands were sweaty. I almost went into a panic. I prayed so that I could calm myself before I went in front of more than sixty people. They all clapped loudly prior to me speaking. My speech was similar to the "Ice Breaker" one that I had delivered at my first Toastmasters meeting months ago, and I knew it word for word. I still stumbled on a few words and screwed up a couple of lines, but I was so happy when I finally reached the end of the speech. Everyone clapped even louder and some even gave me a standing ovation, which honored and touched me greatly. The contest evaluators were sincere and supportive, and I received lots of hugs, love and support from so many people afterward that it was a bit overwhelming!

My second goal was to be a spokesperson for those who were abused. I felt that my past experience could help others, just as I wrote this book with the hope of inspiring others who are going through similar struggles. I felt that if others heard my story, they would have the courage and inspiration to go on with their own life.

To that end, I got involved with the victims' rights movement, Marsy's Law, and the Hawai'i State Coalition Against Domestic Violence with the help of a college friend. She brought me to an event where victims of crime discussed their experiences. It was held on the grounds of Honolulu Hale, our city hall. It was then when I met Marci Lopes, who at that time was the executive director of Marsy's Law in Hawai'i, as well as executive director of the HSCADV. Since then, I have helped with a number of events the coalition has sponsored, including its annual conference that was held in September 2015.

The conference was a huge success, and I was one of four people who took part in a panel discussion attended by numerous people who worked for the state and nonprofit organizations. During the discussion, I talked about my experience with domestic abuse, as well as what happened after I left my husband. It wasn't a planned speech like how Toastmasters speeches are, but the panelists knew what the questions were in advance, so we were able to think about the answers beforehand.

I must have given valuable information to those who attended the panel, because many people came up to me later and said it was a great speech. They were all supportive, and I received a lot of nice compliments.

The influence of the HSCADV conference would extend beyond that day. At an October 2015 fundraiser sponsored by the Domestic Violence Action Center, an attendee named Sally recognized me right away.

"Weren't you at the conference a month ago?" Sally asked.

"Yes, I was a one of the speakers on the panel discussion," I answered. "Wow, you have a good memory."

"It's because you were such a great speaker," she said.

It was then I felt like I had reached my goal of being a domestic abuse spokesperson, so others could benefit from what I experienced. My dreams and goals were coming true. What a blessing from God.

I spoke at another domestic violence awareness event, which was held in October 2015 at Waipahu High School, sponsored by a school club.

I had only four days to work on the speech, and it wasn't enough time to memorize everything I wrote. Part of the speech was the one I used at the Toastmasters contest, with the first half geared toward the students. I was asked to speak in detail about how my relationship was with my ex-husband before we got married. In addition, I had to keep it to just seven minutes to allow enough time for a second person to also speak about domestic violence.

When the day came, I was so stressed out. I kept reading my speech over and over. Then I was told that the other speaker couldn't make it and I would have more time for my portion. It was such a relief to know that I didn't have to contain my speech to within seven minutes.

As usual, I had butterflies in my stomach, my hands

Falling Perfectly Without Trying

were all sweaty and I was in a near panic. There seemed to be so many people at the event. There were lots of students, legislators, teachers and parents present. Marci Lopes was also there, and Pancho was with me.

I made it to the stage with Marci's help and a student handed me the mic. I introduced myself and started my speech. I was so terrified, not knowing how the students would react. But soon I was saying my conclusion, although I stumbled on it a bit. I gave the mic to Marci, ran down the steps and was greeted with hugs and kisses from everyone.

"You were great, Jenny!" Marci hugged and kissed me on the cheeks.

"You did real good!" Pancho exclaimed.

An advisor for the students came up to me with tears in his eyes. "That was such an inspirational story," he said, shaking my hand. "Thank you so much."

It felt so good knowing that I had made such an impact. Later, about two dozen students came up to me to thank me with hugs and kisses.

All I could say to each of them was, "Good luck in everything you do. And go to college right away. Don't wait until you're old like me."

I remembered when I first became involved with Toastmasters, how I wanted to help others who experienced domestic violence by being a spokesperson for them, and my dream had come true. Whatever happened from now on was "just icing on the cake."

Being a part of Toastmasters for the past two years has been "just icing on the cake." I remember when I first became a member of the Waterfront Plaza

Toastmasters. I enjoyed being a member, and I liked the excitement and energy I felt from the other members during the meetings. As a result, every chance I had, I attended or helped out in different activities and events, including taking on an active role in the District 49 contests and conferences. I offered to help in any way I could, because I liked being part of such a "unique" organization.

One day in March 2016, Charles Mole, Jr., the District Director for District 49 Toastmasters, asked me if I wouldn't mind being the "Public Relations Manager" for District 49 Toastmasters for a few months. I was stunned!

I tried to fulfill my responsibilities, including making a newsletter every month. I enjoyed being part of the team and working with Charles was awesome. He was such a great mentor to me and so positive and happy-go-lucky.

There were a few times I met up with Charles to have him sign documents or to give him something important. I even went to a Kamehameha Toastmasters Club meeting. Since I was at the meeting site, I decided to attend the meeting, and I'm glad I stayed. There were many other Filipinos who were members of the chapter. Due to their sincere hospitality, I ended up becoming a member of that particular chapter.

Besides being the public relations manager for District 49 Toastmasters, I managed to present ten speeches at the Queen's Medical Center and Kamehameha Toastmasters meetings. The ten speeches cover one fundamental skill for public speakers, and it also came from a series of speeches that included the icebreaker, organize your speech, get to the point, how to say it, your body speaks, vocal variety, and more. Most of the speeches were from my own experience in my life so it wasn't too hard to write and memorize the speeches.

There are roles that members may volunteer to take during the meetings. Those roles includes:

Toastmaster-the Toastmaster acts as a host, conducts the day's program as well as introduces each participant/member.

Speaker-a speaker decides on a topic and prepares their speeches way before the meeting. Each speech is about 4-6 minutes for an icebreaker speech or 5-7 minutes for other speeches.

Table Topics Master- this person chooses a few sentences prior to the meeting and calls on club members who do not have an assigned role in the meeting. This section helps members to think spur of the moment.

Evaluator-this participant gives a prepared speaker a positive and constructive feedback as well as takes into account the speaker's habits and skill level.

General Evaluator-evaluates all aspects of the meeting, including the Grammarian/Ah-Counter, Timer, speakers and the table topics segment.

Timer-this individual keeps track of the time for each participant in the meeting by signaling the individual with a green, yellow or red light or card.

Grammarian/Ah-Counter-this person is responsible

for the "word of the day" and presents it at the beginning of the meeting. Secondly, the person must keep track (on a piece of paper) of filler words that the speakers may say, including words such as "ah," "um," "so" and "like."

Even though my ultimate goal was to enter the Toastmaster's Contest in 2016, I never pursued the idea, especially since I held the title of public relations manager for a few months. However, on August 23, 2016, I received a certificate for completing the Competent Communicator manual when I was at the Kamehameha Toastmaster's meeting.

One of the speeches included "Overcoming Disorder and Addictions," which was about me having a bipolar disorder, as well as being addicted to oxycodone and alcohol.

Another speech I did was called "Hawai'i's Silent Killer," which was about Diabetes Type 2. I have Diabetes Type 2. As a result, I was able to put all the facts and my experience with the disease into the speech and make it an interesting subject for the Toastmasters members.

While I could talk about what Diabetes is and how it affects me, I didn't say that with treatment and lifestyle changes, a person can prevent or delay all the complications that comes with having Diabetes. Sometimes, by changing a person's diet and/or by having bariatric surgery, gastric bypass, or laparoscopic gastric banding, a person can be cured of Diabetes Type 2.

Since I was diagnosed with Diabetes Type 2 in

Falling Perfectly Without Trying

2008, I've made a couple of attempts to learn about the disease as well as how I can be cured. I tried a number of times to watch what I eat and exercise as much as I can; however, it's hard when my significant other loves to eat.

I really enjoyed giving all 10 speeches, because it wasn't hard writing the speeches. They came naturally. There were many things I said in the speeches that most of the members never heard or knew about. As a result, I'm content I was able to share my stories.

As for the title of public relations manager, I had a chance to continue it for one more year, however, I was unable to. I was faced with too many problems with Remie, and I felt I couldn't fulfill my responsibilities without something suffering.

During the Winter Toastmaster's Conference in October 2016, Charles Mole presented me with a certificate for being their public relations officer, and I received a standing ovation. I was so surprised.

Chapter Nine
Coming to Terms with Myself

In September, Remie kept pressing me to look for a place for her to live, because she didn't want to remain living in 'Ewa Beach any longer. She didn't want to stay there because she felt the owners didn't want her to live in the house she was renting, which was untrue. Yet, I couldn't convince her otherwise.

Despite all the problems coming towards us head on, Remie insisted on finding a new place to live, and my days were numbered.

One week before my radiation treatments started, we came upon a wonderful little house in Makiki. I was desperate, and needed her to move into a new place right away. As a result, we took it, and Remie was satisfied. At least, I *thought* she was.

A week after she moved in, she admitted her worries that her landlord was upset with her because her pet birds were making noises at night. She warned me that the landlord would not extend her lease beyond six months, and we would have to look for another place for her to live.

One day, Remie got really sick and ended up in the

emergency room. The doctors told her that she had a viral infection.

The next day, Remie was a mess.

"Mom, the birds were making noise all night," she cried into her phone. "And, I was coughing all night. The landlord is going to kick me out of the house."

"No, she isn't," I assured her.

"She is, because she was up all night long," Remie said. "I'm afraid she's going to knock on the door and tell me to get out."

Remie hung up, but kept calling me all afternoon at work.

"Mom, you have to come now. The birds are making too much noise," she said.

"What? I can't leave work now," I said. "That's impossible!"

"You have to, Mom," Remie cried.

I hung up the phone on her, but she called me again fifteen minutes later.

"Mom, please come now or else I'm going to jump off a building," Remie said.

Then I got worried. I called Pancho and asked him to pick me up at work and bring us over to see Remie at her apartment. I was so scared.

Fifteen minutes later, Pancho was there, and I got into the car and told him exactly what Remie had told me.

Her apartment was in disarray. It looked like she was trying to put all her belongings in huge bags and boxes. As if she was intending to move again. As I looked at Remie, I saw that she was in such a state of confusion.

She was rushing around like a crazy person, and I noticed that her hair was super short. She had put a cap on over it.

"You shaved off your hair?" I asked. "Why did you do that?"

"Because I'm stressed out, and I can't handle it," Remie said. "You know I can't handle too much stress. The birds were making too much noise, and my landlord might kick me out. Plus, I'm coughing a lot. I want to see my old therapist again. You don't know the whole story. I'll tell you only if we can see her again."

"I texted the therapist, but she said she can't see you today," I said. "Do you want to go to the hospital?"

"What about the birds? I can't give them up to anyone."

"Yes, I know," I said. "Why don't you give the birds to Aunty Lorraine?"

I called my younger sister, Lorraine, on my cell phone. Lorraine told me she had offered to take the birds, but they would have to stay outside in a coop. Remie didn't like the idea, according to Lorraine.

"Remie has to make a choice between the birds or living where she lives," Lorraine said. "She has to make a choice, but I don't want you to get sick, Jenny. Okay?"

I understood what Lorraine was trying to say. I had to come to terms with myself. I had to let Remie make the decision, and I couldn't decide for her. I also had to let her handle her problems herself. I'd paid my dues over and over to her, and I couldn't keep bailing her out all the time.

Falling Perfectly Without Trying

Like my therapist had said time and time again, "You can't keep helping her out. It's enabling her, and she will continue to reach out to you every single chance she can."

"Mom, why don't you leave," Remie said loudly. "I know you want to go, so just go."

I got up from her bed and left her apartment. I finally realized that I couldn't force her to do anything. She was an adult. She had to want to be helped.

In the car, Pancho said, "You can't help her if she doesn't want any help."

I understood that. Still, I felt like I had failed as a mother.

As I look back to when I was twenty-two years old, I was so young and naïve to be a wife and mother of two babies. I was excited at first to give birth to my two children; however, I experienced overwhelming sadness and abuse at such a young age. I don't know how I managed to get through those black years.

While life in the 1980s seemed to stand still, the world continued to revolve around us. While so many things happened, time seemed to stop in my world as I was faced with violence and sadness.

I hit rock bottom so many times due to my ex-husband's threats and interrogation. My life was just like the title of this book, *Falling Perfectly Without Trying*. I managed to get up every single time. Like my mom, I persevered no matter what happened.

If I could go back in time when my children were just babies, I would tell myself, "GET OUT with the children NOW." Then maybe so many things wouldn't have happened the way they did.

Luckily, I escaped from the domestic abusive situation when I did, or else we might have had ended up like that twenty-eight-year-old mother, with her eight-year-old daughter and six-year-old son who were stabbed multiple times during the fourth week of February, 2015. Maybe one day, someone will help that mother tell her story to the world.

But I can't turn back the *tides of time.* If there were such a thing as a time machine, I would surely be one of the first ones to want to experience it.

Even so, my life changed for the best after I was diagnosed with cancer. Pancho took care of me as I underwent radiation, and when it was all over, we became closer as a couple. After all the appointments were finished and I no longer needed to see the radiation technicians, the person who stayed by my side while I ached all over was my husband. I was left with a burned side and sores all over the top part of my body. Pancho helped me while I recovered from it all.

Life is full of challenges and obstacles, but if you are patient…life can turn out for the better. Don't ever quit.

Falling Perfectly Without Trying

At a young age, I was introduced to a wonderful poem called Don't Quit, *by an anonymous author. As the years have gone by, I have re-read this particular poem. I hope that you may find the courage, love, and patience within these words as I have over the years.*

Don't Quit

When things go wrong, as they sometimes will,
When the road you're trudging seems all uphill,
When the funds are low and the debts are high,
And you want to smile, but you have to sigh,
When care is pressing you down a bit—
Rest if you must, but don't you quit.
Life is queer with its twists and turns,
As every one of us sometimes learns,
And many a fellow turns about
When he might have won had he stuck it out.
Don't give up though the pace seems slow—
You might succeed with another blow.
Often the goal is nearer than
It seems to a faint and faltering man;
Often the struggler has given up
When he might have captured the victor's cup;
And he learned to late when the night came down,
How close he was to the golden crown.
Success is failure turned inside out—
The silver tint in the clouds of doubt,
And you never can tell how close you are,
It might be near when it seems afar;

Jenny Duhaylonsod Delos Santos

So stick to the fight when you're hardest hit—
It's when things seem worst that you must not quit.

—Anonymous

Jenny and her daughter, Remie.

Remie, Jenny's daughter.

Jenny on her graduation day, with leis, flowers, and her diploma.

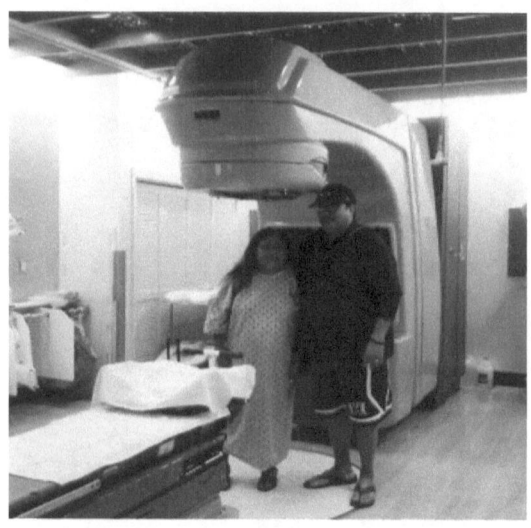

Pancho and Jenny standing next to the linear accelerator machine after her last treatment.

Pancho and Jenny got married on Nov. 3, 2007. The ceremony and reception turned out to be everything that a couple could ever dream of and more.

If you enjoyed *Falling Perfectly Without Trying*, you may enjoy these other memoirs by strong women from Written Dreams Publishing.

Shaking the Family Tree

Dallas H

There was a boogie man in the closet and its name was alcoholism.

This story is not for the faint at heart. ***Shaking the Family Tree*** is an anonymous personal memoir of a recovering alcoholic. It is interlaced with poetic offerings that take the reader to the heart and soul of the ramifications of the disease of alcoholism. Dallas's story is one of coming to terms with what has become her family's unfortunate legacy. She and her sister were raised by two loving parents who did the best they could. As young girls growing up, they never doubted for one moment whether or not they were loved, and were infused with a strong sense of family values.

Alcoholism wasn't a stranger to the family. It could be traced back for three generations and continues to reveal itself in three younger generations of Dallas's family. In her memoir, Dallas explains her battle with co-dependency and the genetic predisposition for alcoholism being the single thread that ties it all together of what made her life a living hell.

Dallas didn't give up. Although she wanted to kick the habit, it wasn't easy. With the help of a loyal sponsor, a lot of determination, and several hard lessons Dallas now shares how she conquered her biggest demons and became a survivor of alcoholism.

News from Lake Boobbegone

Carolyn Redman

Question: Does the world really need another breast cancer memoir? Answer: Probably not.

But writing is the only way Carolyn Redman knew how to process a heartbreaking breast cancer diagnosis and the year-long treatments that ensued. These honest, heartfelt, and sometimes humorous e-mails and essays, written solely to keep family and friends informed of her medical condition morphed into the definitive exercise in self-compassion and healing. In the end, no one was more surprised or more grateful than she was to find purpose and meaning masquerading as cancer.

About the Author

Jenny Duhaylonsod Delos Santos has been a clerk at the *Honolulu Star-Advertiser* for 15 years. Besides clerical duties, she occasionally writes articles for the newspaper. Jenny is an active member in District 49 Toastmasters and belongs to Kamehameha Toastmasters Club. She's also a member of Sisters in Crime-Hawaii and is currently the secretary for the mystery book club. She's been a member of the Hawaii State Coalition Against Domestic Violence, which gave her an opportunity to speak at various events. For more information about Jenny or her books, visit her website: JennyDelosSantos.com or find her on social media.

www.ingramcontent.com/pod-product-compliance
Lightning Source LLC
Chambersburg PA
CBHW030324080526
44584CB00012B/698